The Crisp Approach to

beginning

DOS

for nontechnical business users

by Gordon Kimbell

The *Crisp Computer* Series

Editor: Karen Richardson
Project Manager: Jane Granoff
Interior Design: Kathleen Gadway
Cover Design: Kathleen Gadway

Library of Congress No. 93-70783

ISBN 1-56052-212-7

Microsoft and MS-DOS are registered trademarks, and Windows is a trademark of Microsoft Corporation.

Crisp Computer Book Series

These books are not like any others. Inspired by the widely successful "Fifty-Minute" Crisp Books, these guides provide the least you need to know in order to use today's most popular application software packages. Specifically designed for either self-study or business training, they are "the fifty-minute books that teach!"

These guides are not for technical wizards or power users. They are for the average business person who is not familiar with computers nor comfortable with a particular software package—such as WordPerfect, Lotus 1-2-3, or Excel.

In most everyday computer applications, employees, managers, and students do not need to learn every feature and capability of their software. What most business users want is simply the amount of knowledge—delivered as quickly and painlessly as possible—to perform specific duties: write a letter, report or newsletter; create a budget or sales forecast; set up a mailing list; and other important business tasks. These books use everyday business examples to guide readers step-by-step through just those commands that they will use most.

Concise and practical, the Crisp fifty-minute computer books provide quick, easy ways to learn today's most popular computer software applications.

Other Books in the Crisp Computer Series

Beginning Lotus 1-2-3 for Nontechnical Business Users
L.Louise Van Osdol
ISBN: 1-56052-213-5

Beginning Excel for Nontechnical Business Users
William Amadio
ISBN: 1-56052-215-1

Beginning WordPerfect 5.1 for Nontechnical Business Users
Mark Workman
ISBN: 1-56052-214-3

DOS for WordPerfect Users
Pamela Mills and Barbara Mathias
ISBN: 1-56052-216-X

WordPerfect Styles Made Easy
Geraldine Mosher
ISBN: 1-56052-217-8

WordPerfect Sorting Made Easy
Patricia Fordham
ISBN: 1-56052-218-6

Getting Creative with Newsletters in WordPerfect
Sandy Zook
ISBN: 1-56052-219-4

Contents

	Introduction	ix
Lesson 1	**Using Your Computer**	**1**
	Introduction	1
	DOS Fundamentals	1
	Operating Systems for Microcomputers	2
	How DOS has Matured	2
	The Anatomy of DOS	3
	Embarking on a DOS Journey	4
	Loading DOS	5
Lesson 2	**Some DOS Basics**	**7**
	Introduction	7
	When You Type a DOS Command	8
	Which Version of DOS are You Using?	8
	Changing Your Computer's Prompt	9
	The Change Drive Command	9
	DOS Commands	10
Lesson 3	**Disks and Files**	**19**
	Introduction	19
	DOS Filenames	19
	Diskettes	21
	Formatting the Diskette	23
	Formatting a System Disk	23

Contents

	Formatting a Data Disk	25
	Formatting Options	26
	What If You've Formatted the Wrong Disk?	27
Lesson 4	**Making Copies of Files**	**29**
	Introduction	29
	Creating the Sample File	30
	Seeing What's in a File	30
	Copying the File	31
	Printing a Hard Copy of a Disk File	32
	Speeding Up the Copy Process By Using Xcopy	32
	Copying an Entire Disk	34
Lesson 5	**Using Wildcards for More Elegant File Access**	**37**
	Introduction	37
	Using the Asterisk (*) as a Wildcard Character	38
	Using the Question Mark (?) as a Wildcard Character	38
Lesson 6	**Using the Backup and Restore Commands**	**43**
	Introduction	43
	Estimating the Number of Floppies You Need	43
	Backing Up Your Files	44
	Restoring Your Files	47
	Practical Examples Using the DOS Backup Command	48
Lesson 7	**Limiting Access to Files**	**51**
	Introduction	51
	The Attribute Command	51
	Read-Only Status	52

Hidden Status   54

Looking at Hidden Files   54

System Status   55

Archive Status   55

Lesson 8   **Managing Your Disk**   **57**

Introduction   57

Understanding Directories   57

Creating Directories (MD/MKDIR)   59

Changing Directories (CD/CHDIR)   61

Deleting Directories (RD/RMDIR)   63

Setting a Path   65

Lesson 9   **Tailoring Your Computer's Prompt** **69**

Introduction   69

On Being More Prompt   69

Customizing Your Prompt   71

Lesson 10   **Customizing Your System With the   73**
                 AUTOEXEC.BAT and CONFIG.SYS Files

Introduction   73

The AUTOEXEC.BAT File   74

Creating the AUTOEXEC.BAT File   75

The CONFIG.SYS File   76

Creating the CONFIG.SYS File   77

Summary   78

Contents

Appendix A   Your PC and the Graphical User   79
              Interface (GUI)

Appendix B   Working With Files in the DOS Shell   93

Appendix C   Using EDIT as a Text Editor   113

Appendix D   Common DOS Error Messages   125

Appendix E   Summary of Basic DOS Commands   129

Appendix F   Glossary of Terms   141

              Index   151

Introduction

DOS is the name given to your computer's disk operating system. In this book, we will explore some of the basic DOS commands and discuss their capabilities. To work through the hands-on exercises, you should have a DOS-based microcomputer. Version 5 of DOS is emphasized, but users of DOS 3.3 and later (including version 6) will certainly benefit from this book.

Why Another DOS Book?

DOS books come in a variety of styles. Most texts are just that—a text that requires a substantial block of time to study and comprehend. This book is designed for the person who operates on a limited time budget, seizing time to learn as time permits. *Beginning DOS for Nontechnical Business Users* consists of 10 short, easy-to-understand lessons. The command line or DOS prompt commands are discussed in these lessons, while the DOS Shell and graphics mode are discussed in the appendices—allowing you to learn both approaches to implementing DOS commands.

How To Use This Book

Divided into short, manageable lessons, this book allows you to actively participate by *trying it* on your own computer. Each lesson is divided into the following segments: objectives, introduction, explanations of each topic with samples of outcomes, and hands-on exercises. The appendices and inside cover notes provide you with additional handy reference material. It is a good idea to glance through these before you begin the lessons—and again after working through a few lessons—so that you can use this material to answer any questions that might arise.

Before you begin a lesson, try to set aside enough time to complete that lesson. Take the time to read through each lesson. Then, actively participate in the hands-on sections of each lesson, where you will develop your confidence in using DOS.

Plan on making mistakes. A computer is a tool; as with any tool, it takes time and repetition to become skillful. Don't be afraid to repeat a lesson; because each lesson is a complete and independent unit, mastering a lesson reinforces a new skill level.

Conventions Used in This Book

Throughout this text, certain styles and special characters are used to help guide you through the lessons. Here are the most common conventions used:

Examples

The named keys on the keyboard (such as Alt, Control, and Enter) appear as keycaps.

Ctrl Enter

The function keys (F1 through F10 or F12) and the cursor control keys (up, down, left, and right arrows) also appear as keycaps.

F3 ↑

Key names separated by a hyphen (-) indicate that you must press and hold down the first one or two keys (Ctrl and Alt) while you press thelast key (Del)—and then release all.

Ctrl-Alt-Del

Key names separated by a comma (,) indicate that you must press the first key (F6), release it,then press the second key (Enter), and release it.

F6 , Enter

Words appearing in bold print are key terms associated with DOS and are defined withinthe sentence. They are also included in the Glossary of Terms (Appendix F).

hard disk

Text that you are to type appears in a different typeface.

Type: CD \DOS

Variables within a command sequence are indicated with square brackets ([ ]). You do notmodify it to fit the situation. For example, you might substitute C:*.* for the [source] and A:\ for the [target] to use the command XCOPY C:*.* A:\ appropriately.

XCOPY [source][target]

1
LESSON

OBJECTIVES

- Learn the basics of the microcomputer
- Look at the microcomputer's disk operating system (DOS)
- Start your computer

Using Your Computer

Introduction

Since the advent of DOS in 1981, the microcomputer (also referred to as the personal computer or PC) has rocketed to enormous success. Little did Bill Gates and Paul Allen, co-founders of Microsoft Corporation, realize that their own personal pastime would result in making the microcomputer the familiar tool that it is today! Many of you are first-time computer users. The sea of jargon and wide range of software and equipment are probably very puzzling. Starting with this lesson, we hope to lift some of that shroud of mystery.

DOS Fundamentals

What are the functions of the disk operating system (DOS)? DOS is the most important piece of **software** that you will use with your personal computer. It is the software that makes the computer work as a system. DOS is a set of programs that allows the computer to control and manage its **hardware** and disk files. Much of the work of DOS is hidden from the microcomputer user because DOS does the worrying about many things, among which is the issue of where and how to save data on disks.

Operating Systems for Microcomputers

Your microcomputer can run under several operating systems. We say "under" because your computer is under the control of the operating system. Various software writers decide on which operating system to use when writing software applications. A majority of these applications (80% at this writing) use either **MS-DOS** (normally used on IBM-compatible microcomputers) or **PC-DOS** (specifically developed just for IBM microcomputers). When this book refers to DOS, the commands referenced will function the same in either the MS-DOS or PC-DOS environment.

How DOS has Matured

Since its introduction in 1981, DOS has changed substantially. The original version of DOS, **version** 1.0, was designed for diskette-based systems and only provided for the basic commands necessary to allow the PC to function. Subsequent versions of DOS have continued to improve the system. The following chart summarizes the development of DOS.

Versions of DOS

Year	Version	Memory Required	Major Improvements
1981	1.0	8KB	
1983	2.0	24KB	Support for hard disks Directories
1984	3.0	37KB	Support for 1.2MB diskette drives
1985	3.1	39KB	Network support

Year	Version	Memory Required	Major Improvements
1985	3.2	46KB	3½" diskette drive support
1987	3.3	55KB	Multiple logical drives on a single hard disk Several new DOS commands
1988	4.0	70KB	Support for hard disks larger than 32MB DOS Shell Extended memory support
1991	5.0	60KB	Much-improved DOS Shell Full-screen editor Improved use of extended memory High memory use enhanced Provision for task switching
1993	6.0	16KB	Optimize disk storage using disk compression Easier memory management DOS tools Anti-virus protection New file backup New file or directory undelete

The Anatomy of DOS

This section is fairly technical, so don't worry if you don't understand all of this yet. We'll revisit these topics in later lessons.

DOS is typically divided into three categories. These are not obvious to the typical PC user because a portion of each of the three parts is concealed from normal user view; these are called **hidden files**. The three categories are as follows:

- *Command Processor.* The command processor, **COMMAND.COM,** plays an important role in communicating your commands to DOS. It is COMMAND.COM that displays the system **prompt** (such as **C:\>**) on the screen, indicating that DOS is waiting for you to enter a command that COMMAND.COM will interpret and act upon. COMMAND.COM contains internal DOS commands such as COPY and DIR.

Your computer may use either a hard or fixed disk-based DOS. In other words, your external DOS files either reside on your hard disk—or your computer may use a diskette-based DOS, which accesses a diskette for those external files.

- *DOS Services.* These include the control of the basic input and output functions of your computer (normally called the **BIOS**) and a file that contains the major parts of the operating system and the routines for controlling the information passed between the machine and its peripherals (devices). Examples of functions that this part of DOS controls are creating files, reading from a file, giving the size and names of files, loading and running programs, and so on.

- *DOS Utilities.* These routines make up the last grouping, providing for many of the management functions of DOS. These commands are either internal or external. **Internal commands** are built into the command processor file COMMAND.COM. **External commands** are not resident in RAM, but reside externally on either your DOS system disk or in your hard disk's DOS subdirectory. For example, the disk formatting command, FORMAT.COM, typically resides as an external file in the DOS subdirectory or on a DOS system diskette (for a floppy-based system). This means that, before the file is executed, DOS must have access to the disk media containing the file.

Embarking on a DOS Journey

So you think you're ready to face the computer? No problem; it's just another tool. You mastered using the telephone, didn't you?

Placing or loading DOS into the computer's memory is called **booting** the computer. When the computer is turned on, a small program in read-only memory (ROM) automatically jump-starts your computer by running the basics of DOS to be transferred into memory from the hard disk or diskette in disk drive A.

You can boot a PC in either of two ways. When you turn on the power switch, you are performing a cold boot. When you hold down the Ctrl-Alt-Del key sequence, DOS performs a warm boot or a reboot. The warm boot allows you to restart your computer with less stress on the system.

When you start your computer, you should see an A> or a C> (or A:\> or C:\>) on the screen. Whichever one you see is called the DOS prompt. Notice that a blinking **cursor** follows the prompt. The A> or C> is called the prompt because it is prompting you to give the computer an instruction. The prompt shows that DOS is waiting for you to type in a command, which is then sent to DOS when you press the Enter key. DOS displays the prompt of the **default drive**; that is, the drive that DOS assumes you are referencing (in a command), unless you specify a different drive in the command.

Loading DOS

Now, let's try loading DOS. As you work through these steps, keep in mind that you are in control of the computer and that all actions are directed by you. Although beginners often make mistakes, this is the only way to really learn the system—so don't be afraid to experiment.

If you don't know which of the two types of computers you are using, either refer to the computer owner's manual for basic equipment information or ask someone who also uses this system.

Make a selection regarding the type of computer you are using (either a hard disk or a diskette-based PC) and then boot your computer according to the three-step process that follows. Because you'll need to turn on the power to load DOS, you will perform a cold boot.

Hard-Disk Systems

1. Drive A should be empty and the disk drive door open.

2. Turn on the power switch.

3. If necessary, turn on the monitor and adjust the contrast and brightness.

Floppy-Disk Systems

1. Insert the DOS disk (labeled Setup, Install, or Program—depending on your version of DOS) into drive A and close the drive door if necessary.

2. Turn on the power switch.

3. If necessary, turn on the monitor and adjust the contrast and brightness.

Your computer should respond by prompting you with:

Floppy-disk systems   A> or A:\>

Hard-disk systems   C\> or C:\>

At some point, you may need to reload DOS; for example, your system may lock up (not respond to keys pressed). When this happens, remember that it is easier on the system to restart by performing a warm boot (reboot). This is done by holding down the Ctrl and Alt keys while pressing Del .

This ends Lesson 1. Congratulations—you're on your way to becoming a DOS user!

Some DOS Basics

- Discover which DOS version your computer uses
- Reset your computer's prompt and clear the screen
- Set the system date and time
- View disk file directories

Introduction

When using your computer, sometimes you will want to look at a disk to see if it holds a particular data file. You may also want to reset the system date and time to make them current, or you may simply want to clear the computer screen and start on something new. This lesson covers these common situations.

Before starting, note that you will need a diskette for this lesson. The diskette should contain some existing files (such as word processing or spreadsheet data files). Diskettes containing software (programs)—such as your DOS or word-processing installation diskettes—are okay to use because you will only ask DOS to "look at" the diskette. However, before working with diskettes with data that you might want to use again, it is a good idea to write-protect them before starting (see page 12) to prevent accidental erasure.

7

When You Type a DOS Command

You may type a DOS command in either upper or lower case letters because DOS automatically changes all commands to upper case.

Each line either starts with a DOS command as the first word or the first word is preceded by the direct path to the DOS command.

There are two types of slashes on your keyboard: the forward slash (/) and the back slash (\). The forward slash (/) is typically used for switches, while the back slash (\) is normally used to specify the root directory or subdirectories (discussed later).

When you type a command at the DOS prompt, a sequence of activities is set into motion. DOS first checks to see if the command that you just typed is an internal DOS command. If it is not, DOS then looks at the default location as pointed to by the current prompt. If DOS finds an **executable file** (normally, files that have an extension of .COM, .EXE, or .BAT), it responds by running that file. If the file is not found, DOS then—through COMMAND.COM—displays the message "Bad command or file name."

DOS commands may be followed by a specific **parameter**—often referred to as the **target**—which is separated from the rest of the statement by a space.

Optional switches may also be included as part of the command. These switches are preceded by the forward slash (/).

Which Version of DOS are You Using?

If your microcomputer operates on a version of DOS before DOS 4.0, you should consider an upgrade. Newer DOS versions contain additional capabilities that will simplify and enhance your work.

If you don't know your DOS's version, simply do the following:

Type: VER

Press: [Enter]

You should now see a message such as

      MS-DOS Version 6.00

appear on your screen.

Changing Your Computer's Prompt

The system prompt in the native form appears as the drive letter followed by the greater than symbol, such as C>. The prompt tells you what the default disk drive is, but this form doesn't tell you what the current directory is. To change the form of the prompt to show the current directory, enter the following:

Type: PROMPT PG

Press: [Enter]

This changes the prompt to show the disk drive letter followed by the current directory and a > (that is, C:\> for the root of drive C or C:\DOS> for the DOS directory on drive C).

The Change Drive Command

Often, you will want to change the default disk drive referred to by the prompt. This is easy to do. Simply enter the desired drive letter followed by a colon (:).

However, don't change a diskette drive unless a disk is already in that drive. Otherwise, you will get a "not ready" message, such as "Not ready reading drive A. Abort, Retry, Fail?" To correct this, either put a disk in the drive and press the R key—or press the A key to abort (you may have to press A several times before returning to the prompt).

To try this procedure, put a diskette in drive A. To change the prompt to another drive, simply type in the drive letter followed by a colon. For example, to change from drive C to drive A, at the prompt of C:\>

Type: A:

Press: [Enter]

Try the following to see some examples of manipulating the prompt.

Type: C:

Type: a: **at the C:\> prompt**

9

Type: b: **at the A:\> prompt**

Type: f: **at the B:\> prompt**

Your screen should display the following message:

     Invalid drive specification

     B:\>

The preceding action switches to drive A, then switches to drive B, and finally tries to switch to a non-existent drive F, displaying the invalid error message.

DOS Commands

Several handy DOS commands make working on your computer a little easier. The next section shows you how to clear your screen, set your computer's internal date and time, display a directory, and use the directory Pause and Wide commands.

Clearing Your Screen (CLS)

Often, you will find that your computer's screen is cluttered with information that you no longer want. All you have to do is

Type: CLS

Press: [Enter]

and your screen instantly clears, placing the prompt at the upper left-hand corner of the screen.

Your Computer's Internal Date and Time

This is sometimes referred to as the System Date and Time. This date is very important because all files, when saved, are stamped with the current date and time. On some computers, the time and date are retained even when the computer is shut off (this time/date data is maintained by a small internal chip powered by a tiny battery). In other situations, you will enter both the date and time when you boot your computer.

Let's look at how you can set or reset your computer's date and time.

Type: DATE

Press: [Enter]

DOS should respond with a display resembling:

Current date is Fri 06-04-1993

Enter new date (mm-dd-yy):

You respond by entering the current date with the hyphen (-) or forward slash (/) used to separate the month, day, and year (for example, for July 4, 1993, you enter 7-4-93 and press the [Enter] key).

Now try reentering the current date on your system.

So, how about setting the time? Easy! The only difference is that you

Type: TIME

Press: [Enter]

and your computer responds with something similar to

Current time is 12:01:00:00a

Enter new time:

You respond by entering the current time as the hour, a colon (:), and the minutes. You may also want to enter another colon, followed by the seconds (although most people do not need to keep track of their files down to the second).

When entering the time on computers running DOS version 3 or earlier, you must enter the time in military form; that is, using the 24-hour clock (1 P.M. is entered as 13, 6 P.M. is entered as 18, and so on). Versions 4 and later of DOS allow you to use either this method—or you may enter the time, followed by an a for A.M. or a p for P.M. (a much easier method).

To enter the time of 2:32 P.M., you would

Type: 2:32p **or** 14:32

Press: [Enter]

After you've practiced entering sample times, reset your computer to the actual time before continuing.

Displaying a Directory (DIR)

You use the DIR command when you want to see a list of the files on a diskette. A portion of each diskette is devoted to maintaining a record, referred to as a **directory**, of all filenames on that diskette. The DIR command allows you to list these names and some associated attributes (such as creation date, time, and file size).

This command is an internal command; that is, the program instructions to tell the computer how to provide a directory were loaded into memory when DOS was loaded (when you booted the PC). This memory (often called **RAM**, which stands for Random Access Memory) holds the currently running program and associated documents; think of it as the work space on your desk. Another internal DOS command that we will explore in this lesson is CLS.

Let's get started!

For this exercise, locate a diskette containing data files. As previously mentioned, this may be a diskette with word-processing files, spreadsheet data files, or even a diskette containing software programs.

For the next set of exercises, you should protect the data on your diskette by **write-protecting** the diskette. If you are using a 5¼" diskette, you need to cover the little square cutout (notch) in the right side of the diskette. You should use the small (usually black or silver) tab that came with the disk. If you cannot find it, ask an experienced PC user where to locate one; it is important to use the special write-protect tab. If you're using a 3½" diskette, locate the square hole with the sliding hard plastic tab (you may have two square holes in your diskette) and be sure the sliding tab is set so that you can see a small open window.

Place the diskette in one of your PC's disk drives. Next, change the prompt to match that drive location. For example, if the prompt is C> and you placed the diskette in drive A, key in A: followed by [Enter]. (As previously mentioned, DOS commands may be entered as either lower or upper case characters.)

To display the directory of the disk indicated by the prompt,

Type: DIR

Press: [Enter]

You should now see a listing of all the files on the diskette at the prompt drive location with the filename, size, and date and time of creation showing.

Your screen listing should resemble the one in *Figure 2.1*.

If you were unable to see all of the filenames because there were too many to view and they scrolled off the top of the screen, don't worry; we'll cover that next.

Figure 2.1

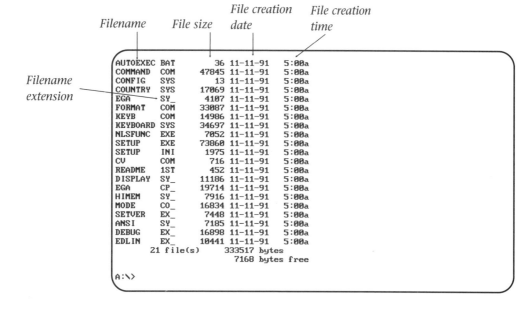

```
          Filename      File size     File creation   File creation
                                       date            time

AUTOEXEC BAT        36 11-11-91    5:00a
COMMAND  COM     47845 11-11-91    5:00a
CONFIG   SYS        13 11-11-91    5:00a
COUNTRY  SYS     17069 11-11-91    5:00a
EGA      SY_      4107 11-11-91    5:00a
FORMAT   COM     33087 11-11-91    5:00a
KEYB     COM     14986 11-11-91    5:00a
KEYBOARD SYS     34697 11-11-91    5:00a
NLSFUNC  EXE      7052 11-11-91    5:00a
SETUP    EXE     73860 11-11-91    5:00a
SETUP    INI      1975 11-11-91    5:00a
CV       COM       716 11-11-91    5:00a
README   1ST       452 11-11-91    5:00a
DISPLAY  SY_     11186 11-11-91    5:00a
EGA      CP_     19714 11-11-91    5:00a
HIMEM    SY_      7916 11-11-91    5:00a
MODE     CO_     16834 11-11-91    5:00a
SETVER   EX_      7448 11-11-91    5:00a
ANSI     SY_      7185 11-11-91    5:00a
DEBUG    EX_     16898 11-11-91    5:00a
EDLIN    EX_     10441 11-11-91    5:00a
        21 file(s)      333517 bytes
                          7168 bytes free

A:\>
```

Filename extension

Using Directory Pause and Wide

Let's look at two variations of the DIR command where we instruct the computer to display the listing of files by using a specific option.

The first of these options instructs the PC to pause at the bottom of the screen display instead of scrolling so rapidly that you can hardly see the files as they flash by—a very frustrating situation when you are looking for a particular file. With your disk placed securely in the diskette drive:

Type: DIR /P

Press: Enter

Your screen should be similar to the one in *Figure 2.2.*

If the last line of your screen is not the same as the one in Figure 2.2 (Press any key to continue . . .), then you are probably viewing all the files contained on your diskette and additional screens are not needed. You might want to search for a diskette containing more data files, such as one of the DOS diskettes, to practice pausing.

The /P in this command tells the computer to pause when the screen is filled—allowing you to view the screen before

Figure 2.2

```
Volume in drive A is DOSSETUP
Volume Serial Number is 3A52-14FB
Directory of A:\

AUTOEXEC BAT        36 11-11-91   5:00a
COMMAND  COM     47845 11-11-91   5:00a
CONFIG   SYS        13 11-11-91   5:00a
COUNTRY  SYS     17069 11-11-91   5:00a
EGA      SY_      4107 11-11-91   5:00a
FORMAT   COM     33087 11-11-91   5:00a
KEYB     COM     14986 11-11-91   5:00a
KEYBOARD SYS     34697 11-11-91   5:00a
NLSFUNC  EXE      7052 11-11-91   5:00a
SETUP    EXE     73860 11-11-91   5:00a
SETUP    INI      1975 11-11-91   5:00a
CV       COM       716 11-11-91   5:00a
README   1ST       452 11-11-91   5:00a
DISPLAY  SY_     11186 11-11-91   5:00a
EGA      CP_     19714 11-11-91   5:00a
HIMEM    SY_      7916 11-11-91   5:00a
MODE     CO_     16834 11-11-91   5:00a
SETVER   EX_      7448 11-11-91   5:00a
ANSI     SY_      7185 11-11-91   5:00a
Press any key to continue . . .
```

continuing. To proceed, follow the instructions at the bottom of the screen and press any key.

Now,

Type: CLS **(to clear the screen)**

Press: Enter

and

Type: DIR /W

Press: Enter

You may use both the /P and /W options when displaying a directory listing.

The /W in this command lets you view a directory by displaying the files across the width of the screen.

Your screen should be similar to the one in *Figure 2.3*.

Notice that the file size, date, and time information are omitted when this option is used.

Now you need to display a directory listing for your hard disk. Assuming that you have a drive C,

Type: C:

Press: Enter

Figure 2.3

```
A:\>dir /w

 Volume in drive A is DOSSETUP
 Volume Serial Number is 3A52-14FB
 Directory of A:\

AUTOEXEC.BAT   COMMAND.COM    CONFIG.SYS     COUNTRY.SYS    EGA.SY_
FORMAT.COM     KEYB.COM       KEYBOARD.SYS   NLSFUNC.EXE    SETUP.EXE
SETUP.INI      CV.COM         README.1ST     DISPLAY.SY_    EGA.CP_
HIMEM.SY_      MODE.CO_       SETVER.EX_     ANSI.SY_       DEBUG.EX_
EDLIN.EX_
         21 file(s)      333517 bytes
                           7168 bytes free

A:\>
```

Your prompt should resemble the following:

C:\>

If you get a name, as well as the C prompt,

Type: CD\

Press: [Enter]

This moves you from a subdirectory to the root of your hard disk.

Now,

Type: DIR /W

Press: [Enter]

You should now see a directory of your hard disk, C. Let's examine a typical screen *(Figure 2.4)*.

More Directory Displays

The DIR command allows you to search a given disk or directory for a specific file or group of files.

Assume that you would like to have the computer search for the file named FORMAT.COM in the DOS subdirectory on the hard

Figure 2.4

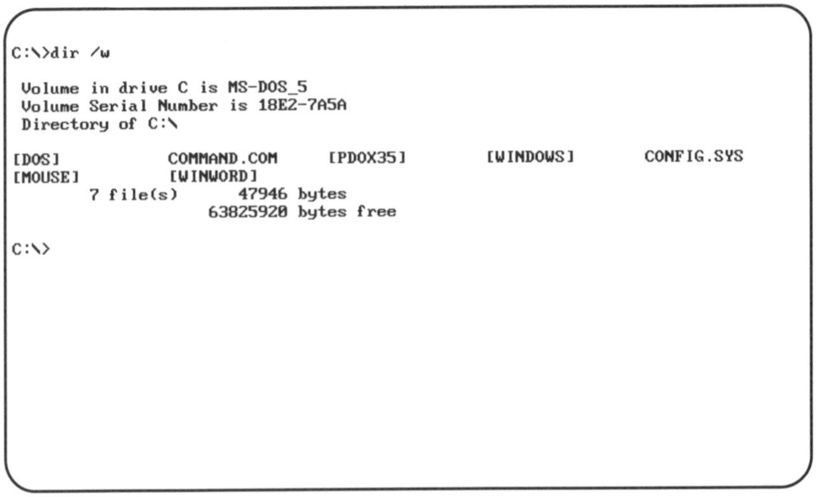

```
C:\>dir /w

 Volume in drive C is MS-DOS_5
 Volume Serial Number is 18E2-7A5A
 Directory of C:\

[DOS]           COMMAND.COM      [PDOX35]        [WINDOWS]      CONFIG.SYS
[MOUSE]         [WINWORD]
        7 file(s)       47946 bytes
                     63825920 bytes free

C:\>
```

disk (C). First, you need to change the prompt to drive C. If you see a C:\> on your screen, you don't need to do anything yet. If you need to switch to drive C,

Type:　　　CLS

Press:　　　[Enter]

Type:　　　C:

Press:　　　[Enter]

This should switch you to drive C. Now, we'll switch to the DOS subdirectory (the location on your hard disk where all of the DOS files are stored).

Type:　　　CD\DOS

Press:　　　[Enter]

This changes you to the DOS directory of drive C. Now, enter the following from the keyboard:

Type:　　　DIR FORMAT.COM

Press:　　　[Enter]

The computer should respond with a display like the one in *Figure 2.5.*

Figure 2.5

```
C:\>C:

C:\>CD\DOS

C:\DOS>DIR FORMAT.COM

 Volume in drive C is MS-DOS_5
 Volume Serial Number is 18E2-7A5A
 Directory of C:\DOS

FORMAT   COM    33087 11-11-91   5:00a
        1 file(s)       33087 bytes
                     63825920 bytes free

C:\DOS>
```

This indicates that the file named FORMAT.COM has a size of 33,087 bytes and was created at 5:00 A.M. on 11-11-91. More information about looking at files is covered in Lesson 5, "Using Wildcards for More Elegant File Access."

3
LESSON

OBJECTIVES

- Learn about diskettes and hard disks
- Format a disk
- Name disk files

Disks and Files

Introduction

It's important that you develop a firm foundation when learning about any new area. With computers, you should have a sound understanding of diskettes, hard disks, and files. The loss of a disk file or a misunderstanding about the way your computer looks at a disk could cause you agony later. But, after this lesson, you will see that the overall subject is quite basic.

You will need two diskettes for this lesson. If you select used diskettes, you will be erasing all existing files by formatting each disk—so be sure that no one needs this data before you start.

DOS Filenames

A file is a collection of related data records that is stored on a disk drive. Files may contain programs (which have instructions for the computer) or data (that the computer processes or acts upon).

A filename consists of both the name—referred to as the **root**—and the **extension**. The following rules apply to filenames:

- The root may contain from 1–8 characters, which may be followed by an extension containing 1–3 characters. If you enter a filename that's too long, DOS ignores any additional character(s). So be careful . . . it's permissible to count on your fingers for this one (even experienced users still do this).

- The extension, which is normally optional but recommended on data files, is always separated from the root by a period (.). However, when DOS gives you a directory listing, it separates the root from the extension with a space.

- The following characters may be used in a filename:

    Letters: A, B, C, and so on

    Numbers: 1, 2, 3, and so on

    Special characters: $ # & @ ! ( ) { } ' - _ ~

- The following characters may *not* be used in a filename:

    ^ + = / [ ] " : ; , ? * | < > \

- A filename may have a 3-digit extension—such as .DOC, .TXT, .WK1—which helps identify the type of file. Specific software products identify their data files with these extensions. For example, the Lotus Corporation uses .WK1 for a worksheet, a BASIC program will be .BAS, and so on. DOS uses the file extensions of .COM, .EXE, and .BAT for *executable* instruction or program files.

    DOS executes files with these extensions in the following sequence:

    .COM first

    .EXE next

    .BAT last

This means that if you have files with the same root and different file extensions, DOS will *only* execute one of the files, based upon the previous hierarchy. So the safest situation is to use different roots whenever possible (if you have control over naming them).

As previously mentioned, various application programs attach specific file extensions to a data file as a method of establishing "ownership" for that file. Some samples of those extensions follow.

Extension	File Contents
.BAK	A backup file that is normally created by a software product (such as a word processor).
.BAS	A BASIC language program instruction file.
.BAT	A DOS executable batch file that is executed by keying in the filename.
.COM	An executable program file typically produced by a programming language.
.EXE	An executable program file similar to the .COM file.
.OVL	A program overlay file used with larger programs.
.$$$	A temporary file that is usually created by an application program. This file is typically erased by DOS after it is no longer needed.

Diskettes

The diskette, sometimes referred to as a **floppy disk,** allows you to manually transport data between computers. The biggest disadvantages of the diskette are the time that it takes the computer to access the disk drive and the limited capacity of the diskette.

The following table shows the relationship of diskettes to size and capacity.

Diskette Type	Capacity
5¼" single-sided/single-density (rare on today's PCs)	180KB or 180,000 bytes
5¼" double-sided/ double-density	360KB or 360,000 bytes
5¼" high-density	1.2MB or 1,200,000 bytes
3½" double-sided/ double-density	720KB or 720,000 bytes
3½" high-density	1.44MB or 1,440,000 bytes
3½" quad-density (the newest)	2.88MB or 2,880,000 bytes

It's important to understand that different size and capacity disk drives tolerate only certain size and capacity disks. What? All this means is that:

1. If the disk doesn't fit, don't force it; you could ruin an expensive piece of hardware.

2. Check the capacity of your diskette drive. You may use a lower capacity diskette in a higher capacity disk drive, but not the reverse. The term for this is that disk drives are downwardly compatible. Therefore, you may use a 5¼" 360KB diskette with a 5¼" high-density (1.2MB) drive. The reverse, however, is not true.

The following portion of this lesson requires that you use a diskette. As mentioned earlier, you may use either new diskettes or ones that have existing data files that may be destroyed.

Formatting the Diskette

Disks formatted by DOS may only be used on IBM-compatible microcomputers.

If your computer has a hard disk C, be careful when using the Format command. If used incorrectly, you may format the hard disk, which can take a lot of time and heartache to reconstruct. Formatting destroys all data on a disk.

To use a disk, you first must format it by using the DOS external program named FORMAT. Formatting checks the disk for bad areas that are unusable and establishes addressable areas on the disk. This enables you to save data files, the filename, and the associated disk location in the **file allocation table (FAT)** on the disk.

When a disk is manufactured—either a floppy diskette or a **hard disk**—it is not automatically recognizable by a PC. Your first step in preparing the disk to be used as a secondary storage (not internal to the computer) medium by a PC is to format the disk.

At this point in the lesson, you should understand that formatting a disk removes all data files, if they exist, on that particular disk. Regardless of the application that you are running, the data may not be saved or transferred to a disk until the disk is formatted. Basically, most diskettes sold by computer stores must be formatted before using.

When formatting a disk, you may either format the disk as a data disk or as a system (bootable) disk. Both methods are discussed in the following sections.

Formatting a System Disk

The formatting process may be performed on both floppy and hard disks.

When formatting a system disk, you direct DOS to perform a normal formatting procedure. However, DOS also copies the system files to the disk, making it a bootable disk.

Whenever possible, you should format a diskette as a **system disk** and then file that disk in a safe, retrievable location. Then, this disk can be used to boot your computer if your hard disk fails. It is also wise to get into the habit of backing up data files frequently so that if your main source of information is ever lost or destroyed, you will still have a copy of it.

Now, enter the following:

Type: `FORMAT A: /S`

Press: [Enter]

At the computer prompt of

Insert new diskette for drive A:

and press ENTER when ready...

place a blank disk in drive A and then close the disk drive door. Next, press the [Enter] key.

NOTE

If the formatting process takes a very long time, or if you get an error message during the formatting process, you should check to make sure that the disk drive and diskette density match (refer to the "Formatting Options" section on pages 26-27 for more information).

The computer will begin the formatting process; depending on the version of DOS you are using, its responses will differ. A typical response is an indication as to the percentage of work (formatting) that is completed.

When prompted for a Volume label, type `SYSTEM DISK` and press [Enter] (you are allowed an 11-character Volume label).

After the formatting operation is complete, DOS will send you a message similar to the one in *Figure 3.1*.

Figure 3.1

```
C:\>FORMAT A: /S
Insert new diskette for drive A:
and press ENTER when ready...

Checking existing disk format.
Saving UNFORMAT information.
Verifying 1.2M
Format complete.
System transferred

Volume label (11 characters, ENTER for none)? SYSTEM DISK

   1213952 bytes total disk space
    119808 bytes used by system
   1094144 bytes available on disk

       512 bytes in each allocation unit.
      2137 allocation units available on disk.

Volume Serial Number is 372B-15F4

Format another (Y/N)?
```

Respond to the last question on the screen by entering an N and pressing Enter.

You should now be back at the prompt again.

Formatting a Data Disk

Your next task is to format a **data disk**. Using another blank disk, repeat the procedure for formatting a system disk, except

Type: FORMAT A:

Press: Enter

When prompted for a **volume label**,

Type: DATA DISK

Press: Enter

Press: N **(to not format another disk)**

Your screen should look like the one in *Figure 3.2*.

You should also label each of the diskettes with a disk label (you should have received some when you purchased the diskettes). Do not write directly on the disk because you may damage it.

Figure 3.2

```
C:\>FORMAT A:
Insert new diskette for drive A:
and press ENTER when ready...

Checking existing disk format.
Saving UNFORMAT information.
Verifying 1.2M
Format complete.

Volume label (11 characters, ENTER for none)? DATA DISK

   1213952 bytes total disk space
   1213952 bytes available on disk

       512 bytes in each allocation unit.
      2371 allocation units available on disk.

Volume Serial Number is 3A34-15F6

Format another (Y/N)?N

C:\>
```

25

Print SYSTEM DISK and DATA DISK on two of these labels and affix them as follows:

- 3½" diskette—in the slightly depressed area on the top side of the diskette.

- 5¼" diskette—in the upper left-hand corner on the top side of the diskette.

Plastic or paper envelopes also should have come with your disks. Put the disks in their envelopes to further protect them. Save both of these diskettes in a safe place because they will be used in future hands-on exercises.

Formatting Options

At this point, it's important to provide you with additional formatting information. Earlier, the book mentioned that you had the capability to format diskettes in non-matching disk drives. This short section shows you those combinations.

The Format command allows you to add a parameter to the end of the command. For instance, using DOS 5 or 6, to format a 360KB diskette in disk drive A in a 720KB disk drive, you

Type: FORMAT A:/F:360

As you see, the F: parameter, which is an option for this command, must be preceded by the / (forward slash).

Other acceptable DOS 5 or 6 parameters for this command are listed in the following table.

NOTE

The /F formatting option works with DOS 4.0 and later. For earlier version parameters, refer to the appropriate DOS manual.

/F: Option	Resulting Format
160	160KB single-sided 5¼" disk
180	180KB single-sided 5¼" disk
320	320KB double-sided 5¼" disk

/F: Option	Resulting Format
360	360KB double-sided 5¼" disk
720	720KB double-sided 3½" disk
1.2	1.2MB high-density 3½" disk
1.44	1.44MB high-density 3½" disk
2.88	2.88MB quad-density 3½" disk

Question: Do I really need to know all these formatting options?

Answer: Only if you have to format a lower-density diskette in a higher-density disk drive (for example, if you need to format a 360KB diskette in a 720KB disk drive). You may need to know only one or two of them—but it's good to understand how all of them can be done.

What If You've Formatted the Wrong Disk?

If you mistakenly format the wrong disk, all is not lost. Beginning with DOS 5, you have the Unformat command, which enables you to restore entire disks that were accidentally reformatted. For this command to function, you must have formatted the disk with the DOS 5 or 6 Format command and you must not have used the /U switch, which formats entire disks without recording the information required for unformatting.

The syntax of this command is

UNFORMAT A:

where A: is the target drive to be unformatted.

If you're careful, you won't have to use this command.

Notes

4

Making Copies of Files

- Create a data file—and then copy that file
- Print a file's contents
- Copy an entire disk

Introduction

It's easy to make a copy of an existing data file—or even a complete diskette. You may want to give a copy of a file or diskette to someone else—or you may simply want to make a copy for backup purposes. It is advisable to back up all vital disk files routinely. Whatever the situation, there are several ways to make a copy of your disk files.

A few notes before starting. If you have a PC with two disk drives of identical size and capacity, you will need a new or reusable disk for use with the Diskcopy command. You will also use a printer in this lesson. You may want to turn on your printer now so that it is warmed up and ready when you are.

Creating the Sample File

Put your newly formatted data disk in disk drive A.

Change the prompt to A:.

Type: A:

Press: Enter

Next,

Type: COPY CON SAMPLE.DOC

Press: Enter

Now type the following, pressing the Enter key at the end of each line.

Type: This data file is a sample file Enter

              created by **[your name].** Enter

Press: Ctrl-Z **(or** F6 , Enter **)**

> Copy Con does not allow you to edit or change the contents of a line of text in the file after you press Enter. Also, you may not change any portion of the file after you press F6 . For instructions on using a text editor, refer to Appendix C.

You should now see a ^Z on your screen. DOS then responds with:

1 file(s) copied

This means that DOS accepted your data lines as a file, saving them on the default drive (this is the drive "pointed to" by the prompt; in this case, drive A).

Seeing What's in a File

Let's peek at the contents of the file.

Type: TYPE SAMPLE.DOC

Press: Enter

Your computer should respond with:

**This is a sample file
created by [your name].**

Sometimes, the computer responds with:

Bad command or filename

This usually means that you misspelled the filename. In this case, just reenter the command. If you still don't find the file, restart the process by recreating the file, as explained in the section "Creating the Sample File" on the previous page.

Copying the File

You can make a copy of any file by using the Copy command. The syntax of this command is:

COPY **[source filename] [target filename]**

The source filename is the filename to be copied and the target filename is the new file to be created.

For this example, we will create a file named SAMPLEX.DOC by copying the exact contents of the file named SAMPLE.DOC.

Type: COPY SAMPLE.DOC SAMPLEX.DOC

Press: Enter

DOS should respond with:

1 file(s) copied

It is important to remember that *you cannot copy a file over itself.* If you must make a copy of a file and save it on the same disk, you must choose another name for the destination (target filename).

Now, display a directory of your diskette:

Type: DIR A: Enter

You should see a listing of both filenames and their extensions— as well as the date and time when they were created.

Suppose the computer responds with:

General failure reading drive A

This means that you either failed to place a formatted disk in drive A or you failed to close the latch on the drive. If this occurs, correct the problem and reenter the directory command.

Printing a Hard Copy of a Disk File

For this exercise, make sure that your printer is turned on and ready.

Let's assume that you would like to get a **hard copy** (printout) of a file. If you are using a parallel printer (normally dot matrix), the target DOS device name is **PRN.** Because you use PRN—the reserved name for the parallel printer—in your command, DOS knows that output of the file SAMPLE.DOC should be redirected to the printer.

Now, make sure that you have an A: prompt. Then,

Type: COPY SAMPLE.DOC PRN (Enter)

This sends a copy of the file's contents to the printer.

There are several ways of directing the screen output to a printer. These will be discussed in later chapters.

If you did not get printed output, either your printer was not in the Ready mode or your printer is not attached to your computer's parallel port. If you are using a laser printer, you will probably have to

Type: PRINT SAMPLE.DOC (Enter)

DOS should respond with:

Name of list device [PRN]:

You respond by pressing (Enter). This should give you output.

Speeding Up the Copy Process By Using Xcopy

The Xcopy command is an extended version of Copy. Instead of reading and writing one file at a time, Xcopy reads multiple files into an internal (RAM) **buffer** equal to the available amount of memory. After the files are read into memory, Xcopy writes the files to the target or receiving disk. A typical use of Xcopy is to copy a group of files—or all of the files—on a disk/directory.

Xcopy does not work for hidden or system files and cannot be used to join or concatenate files.

The syntax of the Xcopy command is:

XCOPY **[source] [target]** /V /S /E /D

- The /V (verify) option tells DOS to verify (doublecheck) the copy process. This option, like the Copy command, slows the process somewhat—but it's worth it to make sure that the copy worked.

- The /S (subdirectory) option tells Xcopy to copy all subdirectories below the current directory. If a directory does not exist at the target location, Xcopy creates it. If a directory at the source location is empty, Xcopy will not copy it unless prompted to do so.

- The /E (empty) option is the way that you get empty subdirectories to be copied to the target drive.

- The /D (date) option gives you the ability to tell DOS to copy only those files created or modified since a specific date. The date is entered after the /D and must be preceded by a colon (:).

The following are some ways to use the Xcopy command.

XCOPY A:*.* B: Copies all of the files on drive A to drive B— under the same filenames.

XCOPY C:\DOS A:\TEMPDOS   Copies the contents of the subdirectory DOS located in the root of drive C to the subdirectory TEMPDOS, located at disk drive A. If TEMPDOS does not exist, DOS will ask whether the copy is for a file or a directory; you respond by pressing a D for directory.

XCOPY \WP51 \TEMP /S /E   Copies the directory WP51 and all of its subdirectories into the directory TEMP.

XCOPY C:\WP51\DATA*.TXT A:\BACKUP /D:3-1-93   Copies all .TXT files created or modified since 3-1-93 from drive C, directory WP51, subdirectory DATA to the directory named BACKUP on drive A.

Copying an Entire Disk

The last portion of this exercise introduces you to the Diskcopy command. This command copies an entire disk from the source location to the target location. (Remember that the *source* disk is the one from which you are copying. The *target*—or destination— disk is the one to which you are copying.)

Three important points about the Diskcopy command:

1. Diskcopy reformats the target diskette, removing all existing files before copying on the new files.

2. The source and the target disks must be the same size.

3. You cannot perform a Diskcopy on a hard disk.

If you need to perform copying for either of the last two situations, you should use the Copy—or better yet, the Xcopy— command.

The syntax of this command is:

DISKCOPY **[source disk location] [target disk location]**

For your hands-on exercise, you will copy from your data disk to your system disk. First, make sure that your system is compatible with the three points mentioned above. If your system is not compatible, you will not be able to complete this exercise.

Now, place the source disk (data disk) in drive A and the target disk (a new disk) in drive B. If you do not have a new disk, a used disk containing data files that may be erased will also work. If you choose to reuse a disk, be sure to check the disk with the DIR command to make sure that you don't erase data files that someone will need later.

Type:　　DISKCOPY A: B:

Press:　　[Enter]

If you have only one floppy disk—or if you have a 5¼" and a 3½" drive:

If you add on the /V switch, DOS will verify each file to make sure that it was copied correctly. This option takes longer than the previous method, but is useful when you want to doublecheck the copy.

Type: DISKCOPY A: A: **(or just** DISKCOPY**)**

If you use this option, DOS will prompt you to insert the source and target disks when necessary.

If you have a substantial number of files to copy, this method will require you to swap disks many times.

At the end of the copying process, DOS should give you the message:

Copy another (Y/N)?

You should respond by typing N and your prompt should reappear.

You may now verify that the copy process actually occurred:

Type: DIR B:

Press: Enter

The computer should display a directory of the files that are now on the target disk.

This concludes the lesson on copying files. Let's move on to the next lesson for more advanced methods of accessing files.

Notes

5

- Use the asterisk as a wildcard character
- Use the question mark as a wildcard character

Using Wildcards for More Elegant File Access

Introduction

Sometimes, you will want to copy or list a group of files that have common extensions as part of their filenames—or they all might have the same sequence of characters at the beginning of their filenames. We refer to this process as copying or listing a block of files.

What if you recall part of a filename—let's say the first three letters—but nothing else. DOS allows you to access files by entering part of the filename. This is done by using the **wildcard** symbols of the asterisk (*) and the question mark (?), each of which can substitute for actual characters in a filename. The two symbols differ in that the question mark can substitute for actual characters in a filename, while the asterisk can substitute for more than one character. Let's look at some examples.

Using the Asterisk (*) as a Wildcard Character

The asterisk makes it easy to reach groups of files that have similar names or extensions. Some examples of using the asterisk as a wildcard include the following.

Command	Result
DIR SAMPLE.*	Displays a directory of all files that have filenames starting with SAMPLE, ignoring their file extensions.
DIR S*.DOC	Displays a directory of all files that have filenames starting with the letter "S" and have file extensions of DOC.
DIR S*.*	Displays a directory of all files with names starting with the letter "S," regardless of their extensions.
DIR *.TXT	Looks at all files that have an extension of .TXT.
COPY *.* [target]	Copies all files, regardless of their filenames or extensions, to the target location.

Using the Question Mark (?) as a Wildcard Character

Each time the question mark is used in a filename, it is substituted for a single character in that filename. Examples of using this symbol include the following.

Command	Result
DIR ?AMPLE.DOC	Instructs DOS to display a directory of all filenames that start with any character—but the remainder of the filename is AMPLE.DOC.
DIR FILE?.TXT	Looks for all filenames that have the letters FILE, plus a single unknown character with an extension of .TXT.

Next, we will work with some files that are on your hard disk, normally referred to as drive C:. A typical DOS-based system has, on its hard disk, several directories. Each of these specific directories was created with the objective of storing software and data files for a particular application in a particular directory. If you have a hard disk, you probably also have a DOS directory where all of the DOS files are stored. These files are called external files because they reside outside of RAM (random access memory). To reach these files, you must give DOS the **pathname** before the filename.

For example, to produce a listing of all files that start with the letter "F" and reside in the DOS directory on drive C:

Type:　　　DIR C:\DOS\F*.*

This command instructs the system to go to the directory called DOS and—using the asterisk wildcard—list the names of all files starting with the letter "F." If you have a hard disk-based DOS system, your screen display should look like the one in *Figure 5.1*.

If you have a floppy diskette-based DOS system, first place your DOS system diskette in disk drive A:. Then

Type:　　　DIR A:\F*.*

Press:　　　Enter

Figure 5.1

```
C:\>DIR C:\DOS\F*.*

 Volume in drive C is MS-DOS_5
 Volume Serial Number is 18E2-7A5A
 Directory of C:\DOS

FORMAT   COM     33087 11-11-91    5:00a
FASTOPEN EXE     12050 11-11-91    5:00a
FDISK    EXE     57224 11-11-91    5:00a
FC       EXE     18650 11-11-91    5:00a
FIND     EXE      6770 11-11-91    5:00a
         5 file(s)      127781 bytes
                      63825920 bytes free

C:\>
```

Let's look at some more illustrations. The following command directs the computer to list all of the files that start with the letters "FOR."

For a hard disk-based DOS system:

Type:　　DIR C:\DOS\FOR*.*

Press:　　[Enter]

If you have DOS on a floppy disk:

Type:　　DIR FOR*.*

You should see only the files that start with the letters "FOR," as shown in *Figure 5.2*.

Now, enter one of the following commands—depending on whether your computer is a floppy- or hard disk-based DOS system (you select the correct command).

Type:　　DIR C:\DOS*.COM **(for a hard disk-based DOS system)**

or

Type:　　DIR *.COM **(for a floppy-based DOS system)**

Then

You could also enter this command by changing the prompt to the DOS directory of drive C by typing CD\DOS and then pressing [Enter]. At the C:\DOS> prompt, type DIR FOR*.* and press [Enter] again.

Figure 5.2

```
C:\>DIR C:\DOS\FOR*.*

 Volume in drive C is MS-DOS_5
 Volume Serial Number is 18E2-7A5A
 Directory of C:\DOS

FORMAT   COM    33087 11-11-91   5:00a
        1 file(s)       33087 bytes
                     63825920 bytes free

C:\>
```

Press: ☐Enter☐ **(after the appropriate command)**

How about that! You should now see a listing of any files that have a .COM filename extension. Try some variations of this one on your own.

Oh, by the way, if you would like to see data regarding the files in a disk drive other than the default drive, then you may include that drive letter in the command (this eliminates the need to switch your prompt to refer to that specific drive).

Let's try this. Place your data diskette in drive A and close the drive door.

Type: DIR A:*.*

Press: ☐Enter☐

You should see a listing of all the files contained on the diskette in disk drive A. By typing these instructions, you have redirected the computer's point of reference from the prompt location of drive C to drive A. *Figure 5.3* is a sample partial listing created by this command.

Later lessons discuss both the path and the directory more thoroughly.

Figure 5.3

```
C:\>DIR A:

 Volume in drive A is DATA DISK
 Volume Serial Number is 3A34-15F6
 Directory of A:\

SAMPLE   DOC        47 06-15-93   3:50p
SAMPLEX  DOC        47 06-15-93   3:51p
        2 file(s)         94 bytes
                    1212928 bytes free

C:\>
```

Notes

6
LESSON

OBJECTIVES

- Use the DOS Backup and Restore commands to back up all or part of a hard disk
- Learn the various parameters available in DOS versions 5 and 6

Using the Backup and Restore Commands

Introduction

It is extremely important to maintain a backup copy of all viable data files; that is, files that you don't want to lose. Eventually, you will need to rely on a backed-up file. DOS provides you with the Backup command as a method to make backup copies of files from a hard disk to floppy disks. The positive side of using this command is that you can feed in diskettes until the complete backup job is done. The negative side is that this command is slow and takes many disks. DOS also provides you with the ability to re-establish backed up files by using the Restore command.

Estimating the Number of Floppies You Need

Before starting this lesson, you should have "a lot" of disks ready to be used as backups. Usually 15–30 diskettes are needed, but this varies—depending on the size and number of your files. (You

Many vendors provide products that will streamline this backup process. They are an extra expense, but the gain in your productivity can be well worth the investment.

should also have an equal number of disk labels because you will be numbering the disks during the backup process.)

You can estimate the number of floppy diskettes that you will need for a backup by dividing the number of bytes taken up by files (DIR C:\ /S tells you how many bytes are taken up by the files on drive C) by 360,000 (for double-density 5¼" floppy diskettes), or by 1,440,000 (for high-density 3½" floppies) and then add an extra 20 percent to this result. (If you don't remember the capacity of your diskettes, refer back to the table on page 22.) For example,

18,000,580 ÷ 1,440,000 = 12.5 (18MB of files using
   1.44MB diskettes)
12.5 × .20 = 2.5 (the additional 20 percent)
12.5 + 2.5 = 15 (the approximate number of diskettes necessary)

Backing Up Your Files

The syntax of the Backup command is:

BACKUP **[source] [target]** /S /M /A /F /D: **[date]** /T: **[time]**

- The source specifies the drive to be backed up (or the current drive may be used as a default), a path (you may need to specify the root directory), and the file specifications (including any wildcard symbols).

- The target is usually a floppy disk drive.

- The /S (subdirectory) option causes any subdirectories below the specified source directory to be included in the backup.

- The /M (modified) option allows you to specify a backup for only certain files: those created or modified since the last backup (this may seem like a routine chore, but it saves your valuable data).

- The /A (additive) option causes backed-up files to be added to any existing files on the target diskette.

- The /F (format) is only used in versions of DOS before version 4. This parameter tells DOS to format the target disk if it isn't already formatted. Versions 4, 5, and 6 automatically format the target diskette if it is not already formatted.

- The /D (date) option allows you to specify a date and only files created or edited (changed) after that date will be backed up.

- The /T (time) option backs up the files that were created or changed after the specified date and time. The /D option must also be specified with this one.

As mentioned earlier, before you start a DOS backup, make sure that you have *plenty* (20 or more, if possible) of diskettes available. If, for any reason, you have to interrupt the backup process, you must start the process again from the beginning—so it will save you time and frustration if you're prepared.

The diskettes will be numbered sequentially because DOS refers to them by number. This example works under any DOS version of 2.0 or higher.

Are you ready?

Change your current drive to C: and the current directory to the root. For example,

Type: C:

Press: [Enter]

Then

Type: CD\

Press: [Enter]

Your prompt should now be C:\>. If it is a C>, then:

Type: PROMPT pg

Press: [Enter]

(Remember this one from Lesson 2?)

Before you enter the next command, let's review several items regarding the DOS backup process.

If you choose to write a number directly on the exterior of a diskette, use a felt-tipped marker and write gently. Do not use a pencil or ballpoint pen to write directly on a diskette because you can damage the delicate surface of the disk.

- To perform a successful DOS backup, you must complete the process. If the process is interrupted for any reason, you must restart the process from disk 01. So be sure you have plenty of time and materials available before starting this process.

- You must have an adequate supply of diskettes to be used for the backup files.

- Before starting the backup process, be sure to have an adequate number of disk labels on hand. During the backup process, DOS will prompt you for the next diskette by referring to it by number. Likewise, if you restore the backed-up files, you will have to do this operation in the same sequence as the backup.

  One of the easiest ways to keep track of the diskettes is to pre-number a few diskette labels as BACKUP01, BACKUP02, and so on. Then, as DOS completes the backup to diskette number 1, place the first label on the diskette. Continue this process until the backup procedure is complete.

- Because this command has so many different combinations (you may back up a complete disk, only the contents of a directory, only files changed since the last backup, and so on), you must enter the command correctly.

Now, you're going to back up the DOS directory to the diskette in drive A. This process may take awhile, so be sure you have enough time before starting it.

Type: BACKUP C:\DOS A:

Press: [Enter]

DOS will prompt you to put the 01 diskette into disk drive A, so follow the directions on your screen.

When the backup process is complete, examine your target disk by requesting a directory for drive A.

Type: DIR A:

Press: [Enter]

You should see two files, with names and numbers for BACKUP and CONTROL. The backup file contains all of your file data, while the CONTROL file contains the filenames and specifications regarding those files.

Restoring Your Files

When you need to copy the contents of the backup diskettes to their original source, you must use the Restore command. Other commands, such as Copy, will not work.

Also, the Restore command must be from the same version of DOS as the Backup command. Normally, this is only a problem if you upgraded your DOS since the last backup or if you are restoring backed-up files from one computer to another.

The syntax for the Restore command is:

RESTORE **[source] [target]** /S /P /M /N /D /B: **[date]**
    /A: **[date]** /E: **[time]** /L: **[time]**

- The source is the floppy or floppies containing the files to be restored.

- The target is the hard disk on which you want to restore the files. You may let this default to your current drive if you wish.

- The /S (subdirectory) option causes any subdirectories under the current directory to be included in the restore operation.

- The /P (prompt) option asks DOS to prompt you before it overwrites a file on the hard disk that was modified after the backup was last performed or for files that are marked as "read only."

- The /M (modified) option restores only files that were modified after they were backed up.

- The /N (deleted) option restores files that were deleted from the original source (hard disk) after they were backed up.

- The /D (display) option doesn't restore any of the files. It displays a list of the files stored on the backup diskette. These files match the path and filenames that you specified as part of the Restore command.

- The /B (date) option restores only those files changed *on or before* [date]. (Also note that the [date] is entered in the Date command format.)

- The /A (date) option restores only those files changed *on or after* [date].

- The /E and /L options restore only files changed either *before or after* a specified time.

Well, it looks like an abundance of options! Let's go ahead with your restore and then look at other practical backup combinations.

Type: RESTORE A: C:\ /S

Press: [Enter]

and DOS will instruct you on how to do the rest.

Practical Examples Using the DOS Backup Command

The following commands are for your general information only. Do not try them yet because they may not work properly; your file and directory names will probably not match those of the commands. They are provided here as guidelines that you can adapt to specific situations later.

To back up files with the .WK1 filename extension from the current directory to the diskette in drive A:

Type: BACKUP *.WK1 A:

To back up all of the files with the extension of .DOC from the directory named SHAREWRE to the diskette in drive A:

Type: BACKUP \SHAREWRE*.DOC A:

To back up all of the files that have changed since they were last backed up—from the entire disk in the current drive (the root directory and all of its subdirectories) to the disk in drive A (this one may take a long time, so be prepared):

Type: BACKUP C:\ A: /S /M

To back up all of the files with the extension of .DOC from the current directory and all of its subdirectories to the disk in drive A:

Type: BACKUP *.DOC A: /S

And, finally, to back up all files from the current directory and all its subdirectories that were changed on or after April 1, 1993, and were not archived (backed up) since then:

Type: BACKUP C: A: /M /A /S /D:4-1-93

This concludes a rather technical discussion of backing up and restoring files. Next, we'll discuss file access.

Notes

7

OBJECTIVES

- Learn about file attributes
- Give a file read-only status
- Hide a file
- Understand DOS system files
- Learn about archiving disks

Limiting Access to Files

Introduction

DOS provides you with the ability to set and look at special file attributes that affect the actual status of a file. **Attributes** are file settings that, for example, allow you to control access to a file by setting it to read-only or hidden. Attribute settings are also used to show the backup status of files or to indicate system files, which are used exclusively by the operating system. For this lesson, you will need the SAMPLE.DOC file that you created earlier.

The Attribute Command

The Attribute command (**ATTRIB**) is used to display or change any of the four possible file attributes of read-only, hidden, system, or archive. If a file is read-only, you cannot change or delete the file. Beginning with DOS version 5, you can also give a file hidden or system status. Hiding a file provides for a certain amount of

51

protection because neither hidden nor system files may be modified or deleted—and they may not be viewed by the DOS Directory command unless you use the /A (attributes) parameter. These files are also untouched by the Rename command.

The following command allows you to manipulate a file's attributes:

ATTRIB +R −R +A −A +H −H +S −S d:**[path]\[filename]** /S

- +R assigns the read-only attribute; –R removes it.

You can set or change more than one attribute in a single command by separating the attributes with a blank space.

- +A (versions 3.2 and later) assigns the archive attribute; –A removes it.

- +H (version 5 and later) assigns the hidden attribute; –H removes it.

- +S (version 5 and later) assigns the system attribute; –S removes it.

- d: is the name of the disk drive where the file(s) resides.

- [path] is the path to the file(s).

- [filename] is the name of the file to which the attributes are being set or reset.

- /S tells DOS to act on all files in the current directory and subsequent directories (version 3.3 and later).

Read-Only Status

Read-only status means that you can only read from the file. Any attempt to modify, rename, or delete the file results in an "Access denied" message from DOS. For example, if you want to make the data file that we created earlier (SAMPLE.DOC—on disk drive A) read-only:

Type: ATTRIB + R A:SAMPLE.DOC

Later, if you want to hide this file from directory view:

Type: ATTRIB A: +H SAMPLE.DOC

You could also perform both of these operations at the same time:

Type: ATTRIB +R +H SAMPLE.DOC

Now, let's make the file SAMPLE.DOC read-only:

Type: ATTRIB +R A:\SAMPLE.DOC

Press: [Enter]

Type: ATTRIB A:*.*

Press: [Enter]

You should see a file listing with attributes, resembling the one in *Figure 7.1*. Notice that the attribute listing displays a letter to the left of the filename, indicating the status of that file.

If the filename SAMPLE.DOC does not appear in the directory, make sure that the directory refers to the correct disk drive (it will show at the top of the directory listing).

Now, reset the read-only status by using the –R parameter:

Type: ATTRIB –R A:SAMPLE.DOC

Press: [Enter]

You should now see the filename when you request a directory listing of the disk (using the DIR command).

If the disk does not contain any files of the type that DOS is looking for, you will get a "File not found" message. You should then check to make sure that you have the correct disk and that you are referring to the correct drive.

Figure 7.1

Read-only attribute

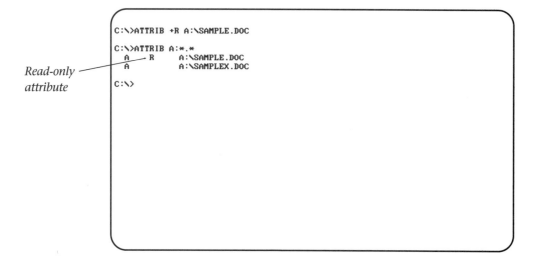

```
C:\>ATTRIB +R A:\SAMPLE.DOC

C:\>ATTRIB A:*.*
   A    R     A:\SAMPLE.DOC
   A          A:\SAMPLEX.DOC
C:\>
```

Hidden Status

Activating the hidden status hides the file so that the filename does not appear in a directory listing. Let's hide a file (you may need to substitute another drive letter for A:).

Type: `ATTRIB +H A:\SAMPLE.DOC`

Now, the filename should *not* appear when you ask for a directory of the disk containing the file.

Let's ask DOS for a listing of the files with attributes:

Type: `ATTRIB A*.*`

Press: [Enter]

You should see a list resembling the one in *Figure 7.2*.

Looking at Hidden Files

Yes, you may obtain a listing showing hidden files—as well as look at any and all file attributes that were set.

Type: `ATTRIB` **[filename] (for a specific file)**

or

Figure 7.2

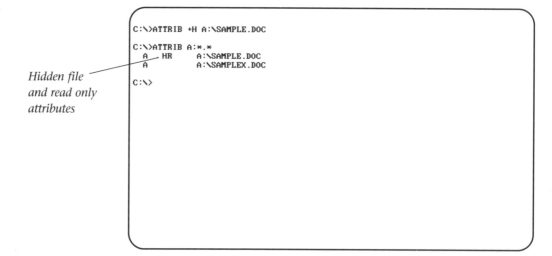

Hidden file and read only attributes

```
C:\>ATTRIB +H A:\SAMPLE.DOC

C:\>ATTRIB A:*.*
  A   HR     A:\SAMPLE.DOC
  A          A:\SAMPLEX.DOC

C:\>
```

Type: ATTRIB *.* **(for all files in a particular disk drive or directory)**

System Status

Version 6 of DOS uses a few more hidden files than earlier versions.

The **system attribute** indicates that the file is a DOS system file. These files include the visible COMMAND.COM command processor and the two hidden files created either by formatting a system disk or by transferring the current DOS system to a disk by using the SYS command.

It is advisable to leave the system attribute and the two system files alone. If you attempt to change this attribute—or if you decide to set this attribute for a file—you may create serious problems.

This attribute is displayed, like all of the others, when you use the Attribute command to display file attributes.

Archive Status

The **archive status** attribute is used to mark files that were changed since they were previously backed up. The Backup and Restore commands use this attribute when performing their routine operations. The Xcopy command also allows you to perform copying based on the status of this bit.

Notes

LESSON

- Create and remove directories
- Change directories
- Specify and set paths to files
- Copy files to directories
- Access a file in a directory

Managing Your Disk

Introduction

This lesson discusses how to organize your files on the disk by dividing them into logical groups, as you would when setting up folders or sections within a filing cabinet. It then shows you how to create and manipulate files in file directories (sometimes referred to as subdirectories). You will use the data disk that you formatted in Lesson 3.

Understanding Directories

As mentioned in Lesson 2, divisions of files within a disk are called directories; further divisions within those directories are called **subdirectories** (although they are often just called directories, too). The reason for these directories is to allow logical groupings of similar data files.

Take, for example, all of the DOS external disk files. You would not want to combine those files with your word-processing software because it would be more difficult to find a file if you needed to search for one. Also, you could have only one file with a particular filename and extension—whereas with directories, you could repeat the same filename within each directory. This is helpful because filenames are often duplicated by software creators (SETUP.EXE, for example, is part of many individual software packages).

DOS also has limitations regarding how many files you may have in a directory. The count is dependent on the version of DOS that resides on your computer for example (for example, DOS 5 allows for 512 files). So, as you add software and files (especially to your hard disk), you'll want to set up directories for these files.

Every disk drive has a **root directory** from which all other directories branch. The root directory is created when you format the disk. The root directory does not have the name "Root," but is typically called that because it is the originating point of all other directories. When you look at a directory listing of a disk, you typically see the drive letter and colon (:) followed by the \ (backslash); this represents the root directory.

Assume that you purchased DOS, WordPerfect, and Lotus 1-2-3 software for your computer. You will probably want to place each software product and its associated data files in a separate directory. Let's look at a graphic diagram of a tree-structured directory that could apply to this situation (see *Figure 8.1*).

In this tree structure (although the tree is upside down), the root directory is divided into three directories: WordPerfect (WPfiles), Lotus 1-2-3 (Ssfiles), and DOS external files. The word-processing directory is divided into subdirectories for memos and for handouts, whereas the spreadsheet directory has only one breakdown for data files. DOS does not require any further breakdowns because all of the DOS external files will reside in the DOS directory.

Before we plunge into using directories, you should keep in mind that setting up directories involves a plan, much like building a house. You must know in advance where the various rooms, or directories, go and where they connect in the overall plan. It is sometimes advisable to make a sketch of the directory tree before you start building the directory.

Figure 8.1

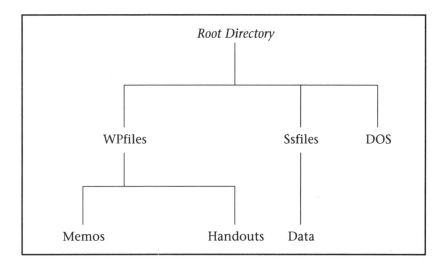

In the next section, as the various directory-based commands are discussed, you will practice these commands by using a diskette as the target for the directories and files. So get out the data disk that you previously used and let's go!

Creating Directories (MD/MKDIR)

Directory names, like the root in filenames, are limited to 8 characters. To create a directory, you use the internal DOS Make Directory command: MD (or MKDIR). So, at the A or B prompt:

Type: MD WPFILES

Press: Enter

Your disk drive should whir for a few seconds while the directory information is recorded on the disk. Now, let's look at the disk.

Type: DIR

Press: Enter

NOTE

DOS automatically converts your directory name to all upper case letters, just as it does with filenames.

Your screen should show any files—as well as the directory name followed by <DIR>. This indicates that the directory exists one level below your current location, which is the root directory.

Figure 8.2

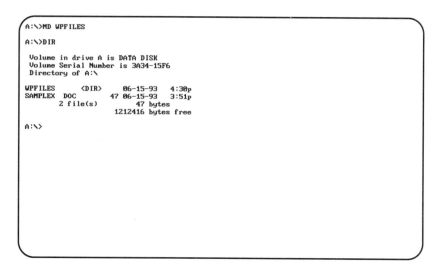

```
A:\>MD WPFILES

A:\>DIR

 Volume in drive A is DATA DISK
 Volume Serial Number is 3A34-15F6
 Directory of A:\

WPFILES       <DIR>       06-15-93   4:30p
SAMPLEX  DOC       47 06-15-93   3:51p
        2 file(s)          47 bytes
                    1212416 bytes free

A:\>
```

Your screen display should look like the one in *Figure 8.2*.

Next, you will create two other directories under the root directory. First, create one for the spreadsheet software.

Type: MD SSFILES

Press: ⌨Enter

Then, create one for the DOS directory:

Type: MD DOS

Press: ⌨Enter

Now, request a directory of the root.

Type: DIR

Press: ⌨Enter

You should now see a display resembling the one in *Figure 8.3*. Notice that the two newest directory names now appear on the screen.

Figure 8.3

```
A:\>MD SSFILES

A:\>MD DOS

A:\>DIR

 Volume in drive A is DATA DISK
 Volume Serial Number is 3A34-15F6
 Directory of A:\

WPFILES      <DIR>      06-15-93    4:30p
SSFILES      <DIR>      06-15-93    4:33p
DOS          <DIR>      06-15-93    4:33p
SAMPLEX  DOC        47 06-15-93    3:51p
         4 file(s)            47 bytes
                        1211392 bytes free

A:\>
```

Changing Directories (CD/CHDIR)

The Change Directory command allows you to move to another directory on a disk. This command requires that you include a "path," which is just a sequence of directory names that tells DOS where the directory that you are referencing is located. The path represents the organization of the disk. Directory names are always separated by a backslash (\).

Let's move into the word-processing directory that you just established.

Type: CD \WPFILES

Press: [Enter]

If your system prompt only shows something like A>, then

Type: PROMPT pg

Press: [Enter]

You have just reset your prompt to show the *current directory*. It should now resemble

A:\WPFILES>

This tells you that the current directory is WPFILES.

It is possible to make new directories without moving to the level immediately above, but the method we use is a stabler approach.

At this point, it is easy to establish another level of directories below the current one.

Type: MD MEMOS

Press: [Enter]

Type: MD HANDOUTS

Press: [Enter]

You just created the two subdirectories under the word-processing directory WPFILES. Now, you will move over to the spreadsheet directory named SSFILES.

Type: CD \SSFILES

Press: [Enter]

Your system prompt should now resemble the following:

A:\SSFILES>

When you typed in the \ (backslash), you instructed DOS to find the root of the disk and then move into the SSFILES directory. Without the backslash, DOS could not find the directory from its current location.

Now, make the subdirectory under SSFILES.

Type: MD DATA

Press: [Enter]

You just finished making a tree of directories. You may view the directory tree if you

Type: CD\ **(to return to the root)**

Press: [Enter]

Type: TREE A:

Press: [Enter]

Figure 8.4

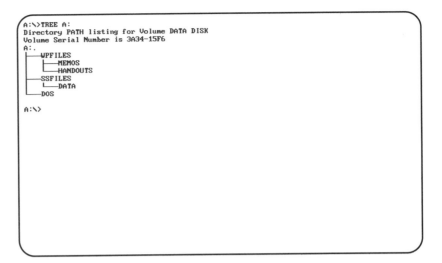

```
A:\>TREE A:
Directory PATH listing for Volume DATA DISK
Volume Serial Number is 3A34-15F6
A:.
├───WPFILES
│   ├───MEMOS
│   └───HANDOUTS
├───SSFILES
│   └───DATA
└───DOS

A:\>
```

This should produce output resembling the one in *Figure 8.4.* Note that this command could also be entered simply as TREE because the current drive is already A.

At this point, we'll copy both of the sample files that you created in Lesson 4 into your new Data subdirectory.

Type: XCOPY A:\SAMPLE*.DOC A:\SSFILES\DATA

DOS should confirm the copy process by listing the filenames copied, followed by the message:

2 File(s) copied

Deleting Directories (RD/RMDIR)

The Remove Directory command allows you to remove an empty directory from your disk. It is important to note that the directory must not contain either files or other subdirectories. If you wanted to remove the Data subdirectory from our example, you would move directly into the Data subdirectory.

Type: CD A:\SSFILES\DATA

Press: [Enter]

Notice that we've specified both the drive and subdirectories as the path. Your system prompt should now look look like the following:

A:\SSFILES\DATA>

Now,

Type: DEL *.*

Press: [Enter]

Then,

Type: Y

Press: [Enter]

to verify deletion of all files in the Data subdirectory.

To remove the Data subdirectory, move up one level.

Type: CD..

Press: [Enter]

Next, remove the Data subdirectory.

Type: RD DATA

Press: [Enter]

Now, let's check your work. Return to the root.

Type: CD\

Press: [Enter]

Now ask for a directory tree.

Type: TREE

Press: [Enter]

You should see a screen resembling *Figure 8.5.*

NOTE

Type CD.. to move up one level in a directory schema.

Figure 8.5

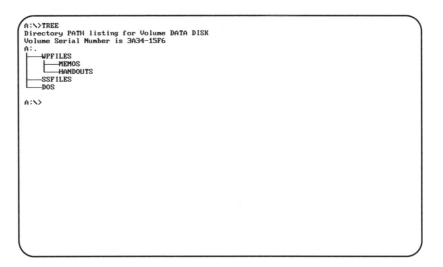

```
A:\>TREE
Directory PATH listing for Volume DATA DISK
Volume Serial Number is 3A34-15F6
A:.
├───WPFILES
│   ├───MEMOS
│   └───HANDOUTS
├───SSFILES
└───DOS

A:\>
```

Setting a Path

After you establish a directory schema or tree, you will probably find it awkward to access certain files when you need to use them. For instance, after putting all of your DOS files in a DOS directory, each time that you wanted to use the XCOPY file, you would first have to provide DOS with the *drive* and *path* necessary to access the Xcopy command. Another method would be to make the DOS directory the current directory by typing CD DOS each time you needed to do an Xcopy. For example, if you wanted to copy all of the files from drive A to drive B, you would have to enter the following syntax:

[drive][path] XCOPY A: B:

or

C:\DOS\XCOPY A: B:

with C:\ as the drive where the directory DOS resides and the file XCOPY as an executable file that resides in the DOS subdirectory.

This is too much work! It's easier if you set up a path for DOS to follow so that DOS can find the Xcopy command without your having to type the klutzy path each time.

The Path command lets you execute commands without entering the pathname or changing directories. The Path command tells DOS to automatically search specified drives and/or directories if the desired executable file cannot be found in the current or default locations (that's the one that your prompt points to). Executable files are those files with a .COM, .EXE, or .BAT file extension.

The Path command uses semicolons (;) to separate your list of drives and directories. DOS then searches through this list in the sequence that you entered it in the Path command when it tries to execute a command.

The command syntax is:

PATH [drive:][path;][drive:][path]

or

PATH

If used by itself, the Path command displays the current path setting for your computer.

Type: PATH

Press: [Enter]

You should now see your system's path setting.

Try setting your path to DOS (you will normally set it to the root of drive C first).

Type: PATH C:\;C:\DOS

Press: [Enter]

Type: PATH

Press: [Enter]

Your computer should respond with

PATH=C:\;C:\DOS

Remember that this path disappears when you turn off your computer. However, you will learn how to set it automatically when booting your computer in Lesson 10.

Notes

9

Tailoring Your System's Prompt

Introduction

Previously, you changed the prompt from the C> (or A>) to either the C:\> or A:\> to let the computer provide you with information regarding the default path. This basically tells you where you are—a must when using a hard disk.

On Being More Prompt

The DOS prompt is very flexible because you can customize it to look like almost anything. I once changed the prompt on my office assistant's computer to say:

Welcome back, Lisa. How was your vacation?

Lisa found this prompt responding to her every press of the [Enter] key. This is okay for a joke, but let's look at some practical options for setting the prompt.

The C> prompt is basically both boring and nondescript because it doesn't tell you where it is in regard to directories or any other important stuff. So let's look at the Prompt command and some of the options.

The syntax of the Prompt command is:

PROMPT **[prompt string]**

The [prompt string] may consist of two parts: **literals** and **metastrings.** A literal is any sequence of alphabetic and numeric characters (such as the Lisa message from the previous example), while a metastring is a character preceded by a dollar sign ($). Acceptable metastring characters are shown in the following table.

Character/Symbol	Produces
d	Current date
p	Current drive and directory
n	Current drive
t	Current time
v	DOS version number
g	Greater than sign (>)
l	Less than sign (<)
b	Vertical bar (I)
q	Equals sign (=)
e	Escape character
h	Backspace
$	Dollar sign ($)
_(underline)	Specifies the end of a line in the prompt and signals the start of a new line

You may include as many combinations of the $ followed by a character as you want. The prompt is changed immediately after you enter the Prompt command. If you enter an invalid character (one not included in this table), DOS ignores the character and continues interpreting the rest of the prompt specifications. If you enter the word "PROMPT" with no specifications, your prompt will be reset to the default or current prompt (for example, C>).

Let's reset the prompt to the default. Make sure that your prompt refers to drive C (if it currently references A, B, or another drive, change it to drive C by typing C: and [Enter]). Now,

Type: PROMPT

Press: [Enter]

You should have a C> prompt.

Next, we'll change the prompt to reflect the current drive and directory, followed by a greater than symbol (>). But first, we'll make sure that the default reference is to the root of drive C. This is accomplished by typing CD\ and [Enter]. To reset the prompt:

Type: PROMPT pg

Press: [Enter]

Your prompt should now look like C:\>. As mentioned previously, this is the industry standard prompt setting.

Customizing Your Prompt

Let's try another option. We'll show the current date on one line and the current drive and directory—followed by the greater than symbol—on the next.

Type: PROMPT d_ pg

Press: [Enter]

You should see the system date (for example, Mon 4-5-1993) on the first line and the prompt (C:\>) on the next. If this didn't work properly, reenter the command—using the *exact* syntax given in the directions.

Notice that the "d" is surrounded by the "$." This allows the "d" (date) specification to be viewed on one line; the "_" indicates that the next specification starts on a new line.

Next, we'll look at another possibility. Let's produce a message, like my Lisa message, in lieu of the prompt.

Type: `PROMPT Hi there, dude. Hit any key to continue...`

Press: Enter

Your prompt should now read: Hi there, dude. Hit any key to continue...

We'd better reset the prompt to something more traditional, just in case your co-workers don't think you're serious enough.

Type: `PROMPT $t$h$h$h$h$h$h$_$p$g`

Press: Enter

This tells DOS to display the time ($t), but to erase the last six digits of the time display by specifying six $h (backspace characters) because the time is shown on hh:mm:ss:ff (two more digits for hundredths of a second). All you really need to see are the hour (hh) and minutes (mm)—and you will probably just ignore the rest. The prompt with the time hh:mm on the first line and the *traditional* current drive and directory on the next should now be displayed, resembling:

20:45

C:\>

This means that the time is 8:45 P.M. Now, let's reset your prompt to reflect the current drive and directory.

Type: `PROMPT $p$g`

Press: Enter

Looks like it's also time to conclude this lesson and move on to system customization.

10

Customizing Your System With the AUTOEXEC.BAT and CONFIG.SYS Files

Introduction

DOS uses two special files each time you start your computer (either with a warm or a cold boot): AUTOEXEC.BAT and CONFIG.SYS. These files tell DOS which commands to execute to utilize devices such as the mouse or any other peripherals (for example, a CD-drive or scanner). You normally don't have to worry about these special devices because when you install each of them, supporting lines of code are normally written to one of these two files by the install or setup program. However, if you want to customize your computer (whether to expedite the startup process by automating commands or by automatically activating programs), then you need to know about these files.

For this lesson, you will need the system disk that you formatted in Lesson 3.

The AUTOEXEC.BAT File

First, a few words about .BAT (batch) files. As discussed in Lesson 3, batch files are executable files; that is, you may type the name of the file and expect the computer to run the instructions contained with the file because the .BAT file extension is reserved for batch files.

The AUTOEXEC.BAT file is automatically executed each time you boot your computer. The only catch is that this file must be in the root location (directory) of your bootable disk. Therefore, if you boot from a diskette in drive A, this file must be in the root of the disk in drive A. If you have a hard disk system, then you'll want this file in the root of drive C—which shouldn't be a problem.

Normal items to be included in the AUTOEXEC.BAT file are routine DOS commands that you would otherwise type on the command line each time that you boot DOS. Such commands are Date, Time, Path, and Prompt. If you want a certain piece of software to run automatically each time that you boot your computer, then you would put the name of the executable program for that software in your AUTOEXEC.BAT file (does this sound familiar?).

How do you know if your computer is using an AUTOEXEC.BAT file or not? If your computer has a system prompt that looks like C>, you probably do *not* have one. Or, if your computer asks you for the date and time whenever you turn it on, you may not have one. But if you're running DOS version 5 or 6, you do have one because the DOS setup program creates it.

What's another way of finding out if you have an AUTOEXEC.BAT file? Try the following. First, change your prompt to the disk drive that you boot from:

Type: C: **(use a different drive letter if needed)**

Press: Enter

Type: CD\ **(to change to the root directory)**

Type:　　DIR AUTOEXEC.BAT

Press:　　[Enter]

If you have an AUTOEXEC.BAT file, you will get a one-line description with the filename, size, date, and time of creation.

Creating the AUTOEXEC.BAT File

For the remainder of this lesson, you will work with the system disk that you formatted in Lesson 3. Place the system disk in drive A and close the drive door. Then

Type:　　COPY CON A:\AUTOEXEC.BAT [Enter]

The cursor should now appear on an empty line, ready for you to enter the following text.

If you discover that you typed an incorrect line, you may abort the process by pressing [F6] and starting over.

Type:　　@ECHO OFF [Enter]

Type:　　PROMPT pg [Enter]

Type:　　PATH C:\;C:\DOS [Enter]

Type:　　DATE [Enter]

Type:　　TIME [Enter]

Type:　　CLS [Enter]

Press:　　[F6] , [Enter] **(to terminate the copy process)**

You just constructed an AUTOEXEC.BAT file, saving it in the root of your bootable system diskette. The following is a brief explanation of the lines contained within this file:

- @ECHO OFF tells DOS to execute (run) each line of the .BAT file, but not to "echo" the commands back to the screen (this would result in having extra stuff displayed on the screen).

- PROMPT pg automatically sets the prompt to show the current (default) drive and directory, followed by the greater than symbol (the "p" and "g" can be upper case if you want).

Easier methods of creating and editing files are discussed in Appendix C.

- PATH C:\;C:\DOS sets the path to the root of drive C and then the DOS directory of drive C.

- DATE and TIME lines allow you to reset both the system date and time whenever this file is executed.

- CLS clears the screen of any leftover output from the previous commands.

The CONFIG.SYS File

The CONFIG.SYS file customizes the DOS environment and activates device drivers (special files) for certain nonstandard hardware devices that you may want to attach to your computer. Examples include running an application that requires many files to be accessed simultaneously or using a special type of device (such as a mouse, scanner, or CD drive). The CONFIG.SYS file is the place where you define these special system configuration requirements. The CONFIG.SYS file is read and executed only when your computer is booted.

For a CONFIG.SYS file to be executed, it must be located (as with the AUTOEXEC.BAT file) in the root directory of your boot disk. Also, the CONFIG.SYS file must be pure ASCII code, which means that it must be all text—with no special word-processing indents, bolding, and so on. Also, the CONFIG.SYS file may contain only certain commands, such as Assign, Break, Buffers, and Files. Let's take a brief look at each of these commands.

ASSIGN   When used in the CONFIG.SYS file, this command reassigns device names. You must have the file ASSIGN.COM on your boot disk.

BREAK   The Break command can either specify ON or OFF, which tells DOS to either activate or deactivate the use of the (Control)-(Break) key sequence. If you want to be assured that DOS will allow you to break out of a program while it is running, use BREAK=ON.

BUFFERS   The Buffers command changes the number of disk buffers that DOS allocates in RAM (your computer's primary memory). The default number of buffers for DOS ranges from 2 to 15, depending on the type and size of your disk drives and the size of your system's basic (conventional) memory. A buffer is the part of

RAM that the computer uses to hold information that was read, is being written to disk, or is being printed. Each buffer uses up 512 bytes of RAM. The format for this command is BUFFERS=n, where n is any number between 1 and 99 (typically 20 or 30).

FILES This command specifies the maximum number of files that can be open or used at any one time (DOS 5 assigns a default of 8). The format for this command is FILES=n, where n is any number between 8 and 255 (typically 20 or 30). When a file is opened, DOS reserves a fixed amount of memory (called a control block) to handle input and output for this file. The size of the area depends on the FILES option.

Creating the CONFIG.SYS File

Now, we'll create a CONFIG.SYS file:

Type: COPY CON A:\CONFIG.SYS [Enter]

Type: BUFFERS=30 [Enter]

Type: FILES=30 [Enter]

Press: [F6] , [Enter] **(to terminate the file-build process)**

Now, let's test these two files. With the system diskette in drive A, reboot your computer using the [Ctrl]-[Alt]-[Del] key sequence.

You should see a prompt like C:\> displayed on a clear screen. The rest of the action has taken place behind the scenes; we can assume that everything went well.

If your screen and prompt don't look like those described, type TYPE A:AUTOEXEC.BAT and press [Enter]. Now, compare each line of output to those that you typed for your AUTOEXEC.BAT file. If the output differs, redo the AUTOEXEC.BAT section of this lesson. If the screen display matches the lines of data that you were asked to enter, reboot your computer by pressing the [Ctrl]-[Alt]-[Del] key sequence.

Be sure to store your bootable diskette in a safe place. You may use this diskette to reboot your computer if you have a problem booting from the hard disk. (It's good protection!)

Summary

By now you should better understand why it is important to have a good working knowledge of DOS. This book was designed to acquaint you with the essential DOS commands and to give you some practice in using them. It is my hope that those of you who regarded DOS as the enemy now feel that this uncomfortable barrier is gone and that DOS is a friend.

In the accompanying appendices, you will experience another type of software operating environment—that of the graphical user interface (GUI). You will learn the basics of a GUI by completing exercises in both the DOS Shell and in the DOS editor (EDIT). You will also learn how to select items by using the keyboard or a mouse.

So, without further delay, on to Appendix A!

APPENDIX A

OBJECTIVES

- Learn the components of the DOS Shell
- Use a mouse to find your way around the graphical user interface
- Learn how to use the Help utility

Your PC and the Graphical User Interface (GUI)

Introduction

DOS provides you with an alternative method for issuing instructions, which differs from the previous method of typing commands at the command or system prompt. You can also use a **shell**, which allows you to choose commands from lists called **menus**, making it easier for many new DOS users to get started. Both methods have positive and negative points. Two of the best-known shell programs are Windows and the DOS Shell. In this appendix, we explore the use of a shell; Appendix B works with the DOS Shell and its functionality. Although part of this appendix covers the use of a computer mouse, you can understand these concepts even without one.

The Anatomy of a Shell

You may have noticed that the **DOS Shell** (shown in *Figure A.1*) closely resembles another Microsoft product, Microsoft Windows (*Figure A.2*). The DOS Shell, like Windows, uses a **graphical user interface**, allowing you to select items that are shown on the screen as names or **icons** (small images) instead of keying in a command. The DOS Shell consists of elements that are described next.

The Menu Bar

Immediately below the screen title "MS-DOS Shell" is a bar with a menu of selections consisting of File, Options, View, Tree, and Help. You may select any one of these and activate a drop-down menu of additional choices. Basically, here's what each of these items does:

Figure A.1

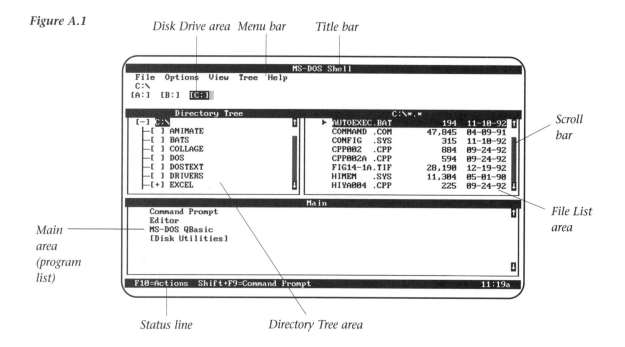

Disk Drive area   Menu bar   Title bar

Scroll bar

File List area

Main area (program list)

Status line   Directory Tree area

- The File menu lets you run programs; give DOS commands; search for a particular file; delete, copy, and rename files; and create directories.

- The Options menu lets you change your display from text to graphics; alter the color of your screen; and modify the way that DOS works, such as prompting you before files are deleted.

- The View menu controls the way that you see items on your monitor. It lets you choose to look at lists of files, programs, or both. It also tells you whether you're looking at files on one or two disks.

- The Tree menu lets you view your directories, subdirectories, and files.

- The Help menu lets you get help for the item that you are currently working on.

Figure A.2

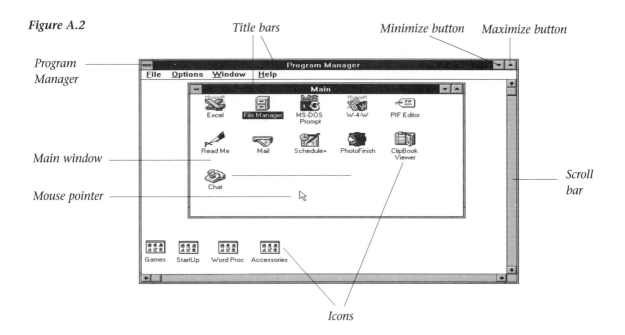

Icons

The Disk Drive Area

This area displays a letter for each disk drive that is active on your computer—typically A and B for your floppy disk drives and C for your fixed (hard) disk. If your hard disk is partitioned (which is done before formatting it), you may see additional letters such as D, indicating more than one logical drive for a physical hard disk unit. The active drive is the highlighted letter.

The Main Display Areas

The Directory Tree area displays a layout of the directories for the drive selected (highlighted) in the Disk Drive area. A + (plus sign) on the icon to the left of a name means that this name is a directory; by clicking on the +, you will see a listing of the files within that directory.

The File List area (to the right of the Directory Tree) displays the names of all the files stored in the directory that is highlighted in the Directory Tree area.

The Main area (at the bottom of the screen) shows the names of programs that were assigned to be displayed in this area. When you first use DOS, it contains only the Command Prompt, Editor (a text editor), MS-DOS QBasic (the Quick BASIC programming language), and Disk Utilities (programs that let you format and copy diskettes, plus undelete files that were deleted by mistake).

The Status Line is important to watch because DOS will send you messages and point out easy shortcuts that you may use (such as Shift+F9=Command Prompt).

An Excursion Using the DOS Shell

You may move around the DOS Shell and select items by using either the keyboard or the mouse. We will discuss both methods in this section.

If, when you turn on your computer, you see the words "MS-DOS Shell" displayed at the top of the screen, you are already in the DOS Shell. In this case, switching to the DOS Shell was probably initiated by a line in your AUTOEXEC.BAT file. But, if the DOS command prompt (for example, C:\>) is looking back at you, then you need to:

Type: DOSSHELL **(be sure to type both "S's")**

Press: Enter

If you did not activate the DOS Shell, but instead got a nasty message from DOS, then (if you have a hard-disk DOS system):

Type: C:\DOS\DOSSHELL

Press: Enter

Or (if you have a diskette-based DOS system):

Type: A:\DOSSHELL

Press: Enter

One of these methods should do the trick. You should now be looking at a screen that resembles the DOS Shell image shown in Figure A.1. The DOS Shell screen is displayed in graphics mode, which means that DOS draws the screen dot by dot. Each dot is called a **pixel**. This differs from text mode, where DOS can only display certain predefined letters, numbers, and special characters (represented by the ASCII code, an acronym for American Standard Code for Information Interchange).

Let's Talk About Using a Mouse

Relax! A **mouse** is only a pointing device that controls the position of the pointer on your computer's screen. If your computer doesn't have a mouse, read on. Computer mice are so popular that you will probably use one soon. If you have a mouse, you will see an arrow or a small shaded rectangle on your screen that moves when you roll the mouse across a flat surface (preferably a mouse pad).

Pick up your mouse and examine its underside. You should see a small ball that, when rolled, moves the **mouse pointer** across the screen. When you start using the mouse, you may be surprised at how clumsy you are. This takes more hand-eye coordination than it looks, but persevere. Using the mouse can save you a lot of time.

If your mouse does not work—that is, if you cannot see the pointer on the screen or the pointer will not move when you roll the mouse on a flat surface—you probably can cure the problem by:

- Removing the mouse ball, cleaning it, and replacing it. The type of cleaner you use depends on the type of mouse that you have. For best results, buy the cleaner that the mouse's manufacturer recommends. Cleaning it with isopropyl alcohol may also work.

- Activating the mouse driver (MOUSE.COM or MOUSE.SYS). Refer to Lesson 10 for more information on the AUTOEXEC.BAT and CONFIG.SYS files.

Let's speed things up. If you have a mouse, you can accomplish tasks faster when you use it as a pointing device. Here are a few pointers on using a mouse:

- *Single-clicking.* Selecting items is usually done by pointing to an item on the screen and then pressing and releasing the left mouse button once. This is called **clicking** or **single-clicking.**

- *Double-clicking.* Activating an item is usually done by pointing to the object and **double-clicking** (two rapid clicks) the left mouse button.

- *Dragging.* Another way to use the mouse is by **dragging.** You can move files into different directories by dragging them. Dragging is accomplished by placing the mouse pointer on the item that you want to move—then pressing and holding down the left mouse button while moving the mouse across a flat surface. To copy the item, follow the same procedure while holding down the ⎡Ctrl⎤ key and dragging.

As can happen when using a PC, occasionally you get a surprise. In this case, the mouse may leave **mouse droppings**. This occurs when you move the mouse around, but still see the cursor scattered all over your screen, typically tracing the movement of the path of the mouse (see how it got its name?). This generally means that the program you are currently using forgot to turn off the mouse. The solution, which you've used before, is ⎡Ctrl⎤-⎡Alt⎤-⎡Del⎤.

- *Scroll bars.* When you look at the DOS Shell screen, you will see several large boxes. At the right side of each of the boxes is a long narrow bar (called the **scroll bar**) containing a small box and arrows at the top and bottom. The small box shows where you are in the list of items contained within the boxed-in area. You may scroll through the complete list of items by placing the mouse pointer on the box, holding down the left mouse key, and dragging the box by using either an upward or downward motion. This action should allow you to **scroll** through the list of items contained within the box. You may also single-click on either arrow to scroll through the list.

Moving Around

You can move around the DOS Shell screen in several ways. Next, we will cover box jumping, switching items, and activating the Menu bar.

Box Jumping

This expression refers to moving the cursor from one box to another. Your first task will normally be that of getting into the right section or box.

To move from box to box with a mouse, you simply point at a box heading and single-click on that item. This should result in highlighting the selected box's title bar.

You can accomplish the same thing with your keyboard by using the Tab key. To move from one of the major box areas in a clockwise direction, you use the Tab key; you use the Shift-Tab key combination to move in a counter-clockwise motion.

Let's try this first with the mouse. With the mouse pointer on the Directory Tree title box,

Click: the left mouse button (once)

The title box of the Directory Tree should be highlighted.

Now, let's try it with the keyboard:

Press: Tab

Notice that the File List title bar is highlighted. Now,

Press: Tab

The Main title bar should now be highlighted. Next, hold down the Shift key and

Press: Tab

This should move your box selection counter-clockwise, back to the File List box.

Switching Items

After you are in your selected box, you can use the arrow keys or the mouse to change items. The active item will also be highlighted.

Using the mouse,

Move: **to the second item in the File List block**

Click: **the left mouse button (once)**

The filename should be highlighted, indicating a selected item. Now, let's try it without the mouse.

Press: ↓ **(twice)**

You should see the selection move two items down the list.

Activating the Menu Bar

Do not be concerned about all of these menu choices; they will make sense in time and with practice.

Now you can activate the Menu bar by pressing the Alt key. Notice that the first word, "File," is highlighted. You may move from item to item in the Menu bar by using the left and right directional arrows. After you land on the correct menu selection, press the Enter key and a drop-down menu of additional selections appears. You may also activate any Menu bar item by pressing the key for the letter that is highlighted (such as the **F** in the word **F**ile).

Now, let's try activating the Menu bar:

Press: Alt **(to activate the Menu bar)**

Figure A.3

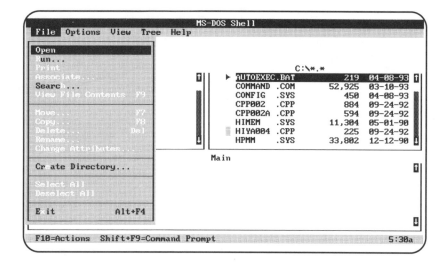

After the word "File" is highlighted,

Press: [Enter]

, You should see a drop-down menu, as *Figure A.3* illustrates.

Press: [→] **(to move across the Menu bar)**

Notice the different adjacent drop-down menus—one for each major item. Any major menu item may be selected by holding down the [Alt] key and pressing the highlighted letter of the desired menu item.

Press: [Esc] **(to deactivate the Menu bar)**

Dialog Boxes

A **dialog box** sometimes appears to prompt you for more information. You can determine if a dialog box will be displayed because commands that require more information have an ellipsis (...) after them. Let's look at some of the special symbols commonly used in a shell:

Menu Convention	Meaning
Dimmed (or not visible) command	You currently may not use the command because it is inactive.
An ellipsis (...) following a command	A dialog box appears when you choose the command. The dialog box contains options that you need to select before continuing.
A check mark (✓) next to a command	The command is in effect. When you remove the check mark (by selecting the command), the command is no longer applicable.
A key combination next to a command	The key combination is a shortcut for the command. You may use the key combination to choose the command.
A triangle (➤) next to a command	When you choose this command, a drop-down or cascading menu appears, listing additional options.

More on the Dialog Box

From the Options menu, choose the File Display Options to show the dialog box that *Figure A.4* displays.

Dialog boxes can have one or more of the following:

- **Text boxes.** You type information as requested by the DOS Shell (such as a filename).

- **List boxes.** These provide you with a list of items, such as file-names—allowing you to select one or many from the list.

- **Option buttons.** These are small oval buttons displaying options for you to select. You normally select a button by single-clicking on the oval. A small black dot indicates that the button option is active. A second click on the button deacti-vates the option.

- **Check boxes.** These are square boxes that allow you to make one or more selections. For example, in the File Display

Figure A.4

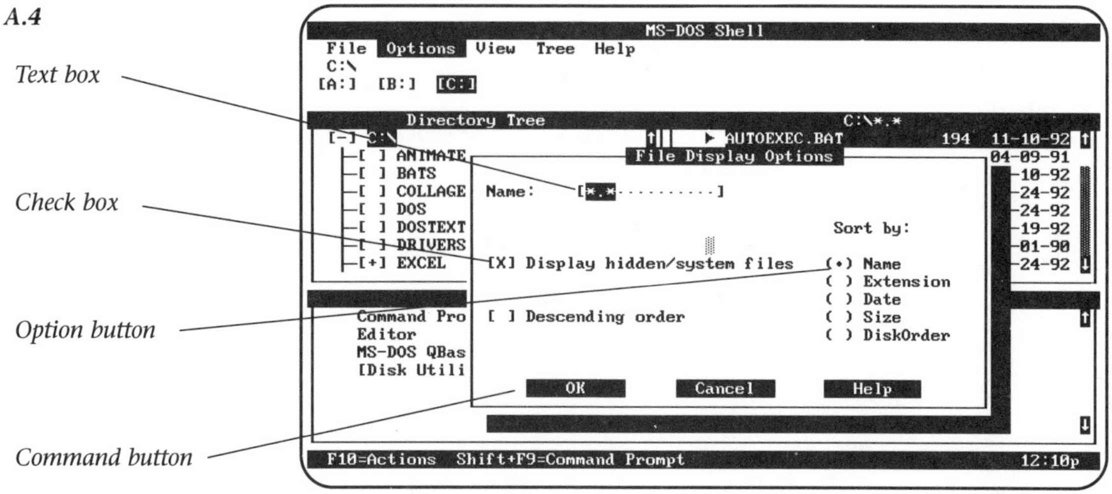

Text box

Check box

Option button

Command button

```
                           MS-DOS Shell
   File  Options  View   Tree  Help
   C:\
   [A:]   [B:]   [C:]
          Directory Tree                              C:\*.*
   [-] C:\                              ↑    ► AUTOEXEC.BAT        194  11-10-92 ↑
     ─[ ] ANIMATE          ┌──────────File Display Options──────────┐  04-09-91
     ─[ ] BATS             │                                        │  -10-92
     ─[ ] COLLAGE          │ Name:    [*.* . . . . . . . . .]       │  -24-92
     ─[ ] DOS              │                                        │  -24-92
     ─[ ] DOSTEXT          │                              Sort by:  │  -19-92
     ─[ ] DRIVERS          │                                        │  -01-90
     ─[+] EXCEL            │ [X] Display hidden/system files (•) Name│  -24-92
                           │                                ( ) Extension
                           │                                ( ) Date
     Command Pro           │ [ ] Descending order           ( ) Size     ↑
     Editor                │                                ( ) DiskOrder
     MS-DOS QBas           │                                        │
     [Disk Utili           │   ┌─────OK─────┐ ┌───Cancel───┐ ┌──Help──┐
                           └────────────────────────────────────────┘
                                                                        ↓
   F10=Actions   Shift+F9=Command Prompt                           12:10p
```

Options dialog box of the DOS Shell (refer to Figure A.4), you can select both the Display Hidden/System Files and the Descending Order options by single-clicking on each check box. When activated, a check box contains an X. The boxes are also deactivated by single-clicking on an active box.

- **Command buttons.** These buttons—such as OK, Cancel, and Help—allow you to tell the DOS Shell what to do next.

Now, let's change the way in which we view the screen information:

Press: Esc (to exit the menu)

Press: Alt -V

This displays the drop-down View menu, as seen in *Figure A.5*.

Press: A (to choose all files)

Your screen should change to an All Files view (*Figure A.6*).

Now, let's restore the screen view.

Select: Alt -**View (or single-click on View if you have a mouse)**

Select: **Program/File Lists (or press F)**

Press: Tab (to select the Directory Tree)

Figure A.5

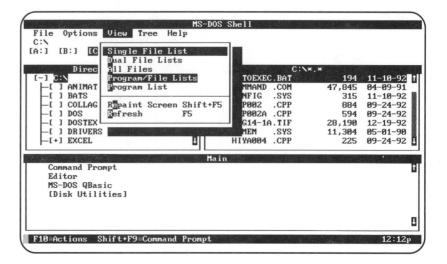

Figure A.6

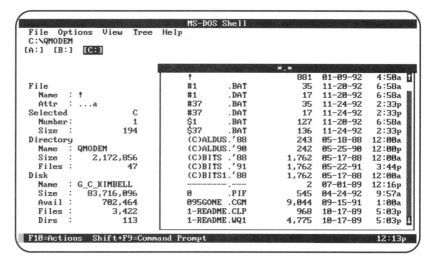

Press: [Alt]-F (to display the drop-down File menu)

Note that most of the items on the File menu are dimmed. This means that they are currently unavailable. For example, Print is unavailable because a specific file is not selected for printing; DOS will not attempt to print a complete directory.

If you want, single-click on the Print option (or press P) to choose Print; nothing will happen because this item is currently inactive.

Press: [Esc] (to remove the File menu from the screen)

Now, select a file from the File List box (remember—you may press $\boxed{\text{Tab}}$ to move to the right).

Press: $\boxed{\text{Alt}}$-F

You should now see that the Print option is available because you selected a single file to print.

Press: $\boxed{\text{Esc}}$ **to exit the menu**

Asking for Help While in the Shell

The DOS Shell Help utility is a quick reference that provides help about the shell at any time. It is **context sensitive**—meaning that it is sensitive to the task that you are currently performing and provides on-line help. To activate the Help utility, simply press the $\boxed{\text{F1}}$ key. You may also request help on any menu item by highlighting that item on the Menu bar and pressing the $\boxed{\text{F1}}$ key. You can get help on any of the following items from the Menu bar: Index, Keyboard, Shell Basics, Commands, Procedures, and Using Help.

Press: $\boxed{\text{F1}}$ **or single-click the mouse (to activate the Help menu)**

Press: $\boxed{\downarrow}$ **(to browse)**

Press: $\boxed{\text{Esc}}$ **(to clear the screen)**

One last item: To leave the DOS Shell and return to the DOS command line, simply press $\boxed{\text{F3}}$ or choose Exit from the File menu. To reactivate the shell, type DOSSHELL $\boxed{\text{Enter}}$.

Well, that was a rather lengthy lesson. Congratulations on completing it! If you are still a bit unsure about the DOS Shell, refer to the next appendix (Appendix B), which covers it in more detail.

Notes

APPENDIX

OBJECTIVES

- Select drives, directories, and files
- Create and name directories
- Copy, rename, and move files
- Delete files and directories
- View a file's contents

Working With Files in the DOS Shell (DOSSHELL)

Introduction

After you have learned how to use a graphical user interface (GUI), such as the DOS Shell, you'll find that working on your PC will become much easier. Because we have already discussed the basics of GUIs and the DOS Shell, we'll now spend some time moving, copying, and deleting files. We'll find out how quick and easy it is to view a file's contents. We'll also rename a file and delete files and directories using the DOS Shell.

Before we begin, those using a disk-based system will need a formatted disk in order to follow all the instructions in this appendix. You may either use the data disk from Lesson 3 or follow Lesson 3's instructions to create a newly formatted disk.

A Few Words of Advice Before We Start

Like most tasks, it's important to build a good foundation before you continue with the next phase of a project. This holds true in working with the PC; it is *very* important for you to understand the basics before moving to the intermediate level. So what does this mean? Simply—it's better to work through the previous appendix before you attempt this one. Don't shortcut yourself; your learning is too important.

Selecting Drives and Directories

The DOS Shell allows you to display a drive's contents with ease. Let's take a few moments to look at your hard disk—or, if you have a disk-based system, a disk drive.

Type: DOSSHELL

Press: [Enter]

Next, let's select drive C using just the keyboard (if you have a mouse, you can click on the C drive).

Press: [Tab] **(until you are in the Disk Drive area)**

Press: [←] **and** [→] **(as needed—to highlight the drive)**

Press: [Enter]

Select the Directory Tree area by tabbing or clicking. Select the DOS (or some other) directory. Note that the names of the files in that directory are displayed in the File List area of your screen. Compare your screen to the sample screen in *Figure B.1.*

You may notice that some of the directory names are preceded by the [+] sign (see the EXCEL directory in Figure B.1). This sign indicates that the directory has at least one subdirectory. To display the subdirectory, simply click on the [+] sign and it changes to a [–] sign. You'll also see a display of the names of all subdirectories that appear within the EXCEL directory. Take a few minutes to browse through your own directory.

Figure B.1

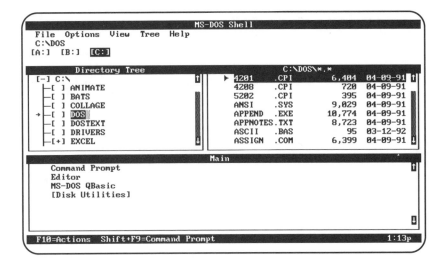

Selecting Files

Now, let's look at several methods that you can use to select files for copying, moving, and other tasks.

Selecting Sequential Files

To select sequential files, using a keyboard:

Press:	Tab **(until the Directory Tree title box is highlighted)**
Press:	↑ **(until the C:\ is highlighted)**
Select:	**File Display Options (from the Options menu)**
Type:	∗ . ∗ Enter

Now select the first three files in the File List area:

Press:	Tab **(until you are at the File List area)**
Press:	Home **(to go to the top of the File List)**
Press:	Shift **and hold it down while pressing** ↓ **twice**

To select sequential files, using a mouse:

Click:	**on C:\ in the Directory Tree area (to return to the root of drive C)**
Select:	**File Display Options (from the Options menu)**
Type:	*.*
Click:	**on <OK>**
Press:	Tab **(until you are at the File List area)**
Press:	Home **(to go to the top of the File List)**
Press:	Shift **and hold it down while clicking on the third file in the list**

Either procedure displays a screen resembling *Figure B.2*.

Selecting Nonsequential Files

We'll select the first and third files from the same directory, using the keyboard:

Press:	Home **(to move to the top of the File List)**
Press:	Shift - F8

Figure B.2

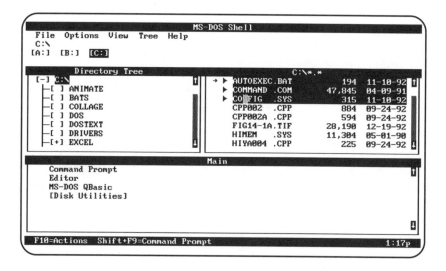

Figure B.3

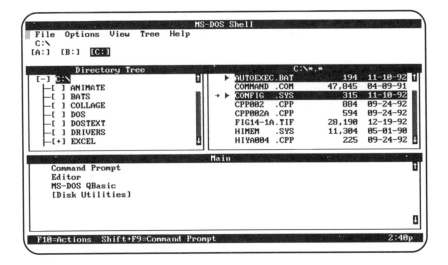

You are now in the Add mode; notice the word "ADD" in the bottom right-hand corner of your screen.

Press: ⬇ (twice, to select the third filename)

Press: Spacebar (to select the third file)

Press: Shift-F8 (to turn off the Add mode)

Your screen should look like the one in *Figure B.3*.

Now, let's perform the same feat using a mouse:

Press: ⬆ (until the first file is selected)

Press: Ctrl and hold it down while clicking on the third filename

You should now see a screen resembling Figure B.3.

You can select or deselect all files by choosing Select All or Deselect All from the File menu.

Creating and Naming Directories

The reason you create directories is to help organize your files, so you should consider the overall organization of your files before creating a new directory.

Each disk drive has a root from which all other directories branch. You may create one or more subdirectories beneath the root, as discussed in Lesson 8. Subdirectories can branch from directories, much like the organization chart of an average corporation. As mentioned previously, subdirectories are often just called directories—no matter what their level is.

When using the DOS Shell, you will find that creating a directory is a simple procedure. To see how easy it is, we'll create a new directory called BASIC, one level below the root of drive C (or on a floppy if you are using a disk-based system). If you are not already in the DOS Shell, activate it now.

Type:	DOSSHELL
Press:	Enter

If you are using the keyboard,

Press:	← or → (to select the disk drive of your choice)
Press:	Enter
Press:	Tab (to move to the Directory Tree box)

If you have a mouse,

Click:	on C:\ in the Directory Tree area (if you have a hard disk; otherwise, click on the disk drive of your choice)

Choose the Create Directory command (from the File menu) by either pointing and clicking on File or:

Press:	Alt
Press:	Enter
Select:	**Create Directory**
Press:	Enter
Type:	BASIC **(in the text dialog box)**
Press:	Enter **(or click on <OK>)**

The newly created directory will appear in the Directory Tree area as a new directory branching from the root directory. Your screen

Figure B.4

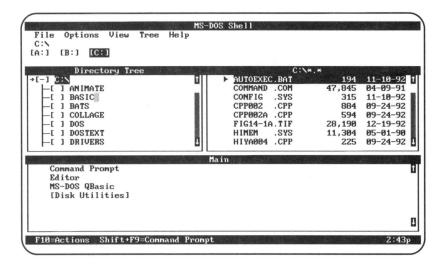

should resemble the one in *Figure B.4.* Especially notice the BASIC directory location in the Directory Tree area.

Next, either click on (or use ↓ to highlight) BASIC in the Directory Tree area. You should see the message "No files in selected directory" appear in the File List area, verifying that your newly created directory is empty.

Now, let's create another directory, one level below the BASIC directory, called FILES.

Make sure that BASIC is highlighted (you may either click on it or press Tab until you're in the Directory Tree area, and use the arrow keys to highlight it).

Select: **Create Directory command (from the File menu)**

Notice that the dialog box has a parent name of C:\BASIC. This means that you are about to create a new child directory one level below the C:\BASIC directory. It is *very* important to check the parent before creating a child. If this is not done correctly, you may create another directory at the same level as the parent, BASIC.

Type: FILES **(in the text dialog box)**

Press: Enter **(or click on <OK>)**

Figure B.5

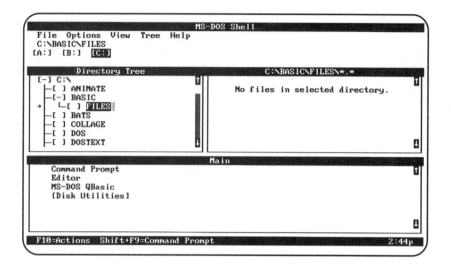

The newly created directory will appear in the Directory Tree area as a new directory branching from the root directory. Your screen should resemble the one in *Figure B.5*. Notice the FILES directory location in the Directory Tree area.

Now, we're going to compress the Directory Tree. If you have a mouse,

Click: on the [–] to the left of C:\ (or the drive you choose) in the Directory Tree area

If you are using the keyboard,

Press: [Alt]

Press: T **(for Tree)**

Select: **Collapse Branch**

Press: [Enter]

Notice the compressed view of the drive (*Figure B.6*). Also notice that you now have a [+] to the left of the drive letter. This [+] symbol indicates that the view is compressed.

Next, let's expand the Tree. With the mouse,

Click: on the [+] to the left of the C:\

Figure B.6

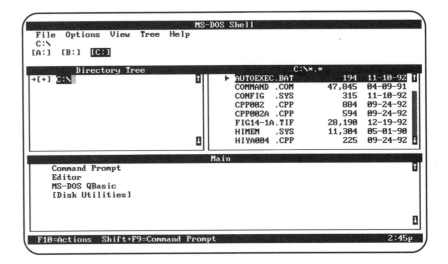

Notice how the Tree expands.

Click: **on the [+] to the left of BASIC (to completely expand the view of the Directory Tree)**

Using the keyboard,

Press: Alt

Press: T **(for Tree)**

Press: A **(for Expand All)**

Be careful not to delete these directories; we will use them later for file copying.

Copying and Moving a File

The two most recent versions of MS-DOS (versions 5 and 6) provide you with a simplified method for both copying and moving files when you are working within the DOS Shell.

Copying Files

Copying files simply involves creating a duplicate of a file on another diskette or in another directory. You might use this procedure when you want to back up a file (also called archiving).

101

However, making a duplicate copy of a file, unless for archiving purposes, can be risky. For example, you might change one file and then forget to make the same changes on the copy. So most users just rely on their copies for backup purposes.

Let's copy a few files to see how easy it is. We'll copy all of the files in the DOS directory on drive C, with an extension of .BAS. These are BASIC language programs (like GORILLA.BAS and some other wild programs). You may use either your mouse or the keyboard to complete these steps.

Select: the DOS directory (in the Directory Tree area)

Select: the File List area

Select: File Display Options (from the Options menu)

The File Display Options dialog box shows the wildcards of *.* following Name:, which means that you'll see all files, regardless of filename and extension.

Type: *.BAS (in the text box)

Press: Enter (to select all of the BASIC programming language files)

Your screen should look like the one in *Figure B.7*.

Figure B.7

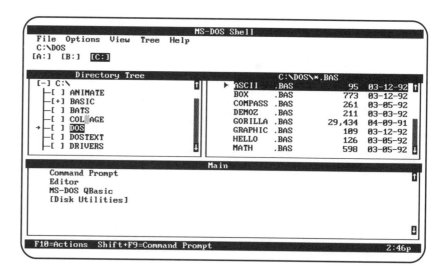

Now, select the Files List area. You will have to select *all* of the files with a .BAS extension, which is done by choosing Select All from the File menu.

Next, you must give the DOS Shell the target or destination for the files. You do this by choosing Copy from the File menu. You should now see a dialog box that looks like the one in *Figure B.8*.

Type: C:\BASIC\FILES **(in the To: target text box)**

Press: ⌨ Enter

Check to see that the copying took place by selecting C: (or your drive) in the Drive Selection area, clicking on the [+] to the left of the BASIC directory, and clicking on FILES in the Directory Tree area. The BASIC files should be displayed in the File List area and your screen should look like the one in *Figure B.9*.

Moving Files

This involves a process identical to that of copying files, except that you select Move instead of Copy from the File menu. The basic procedure is as follows:

- Select the file or files to be moved from the File List area.

- Choose Move from the File menu.

If, after completing these steps, your screen does not look similar to the one in Figure B.9, you probably did not select all the .BAS files. Try it again.

Figure B.8

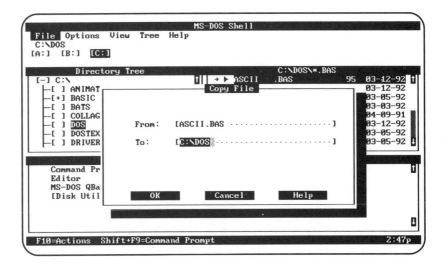

Figure B.9

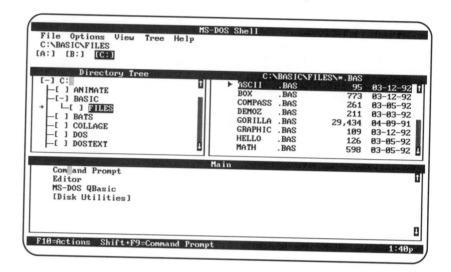

- Type the destination or target location.

- Verify that the move took place by selecting the destination (target) drive or directory.

Let's move all of the BASIC files from C:\BASIC\FILES to the BASIC directory (we'll remove the FILES directory later).

Select:	drive C (from the Drive Select area)
Select:	the Directory Tree area
Select:	the FILES directory (in the Directory Tree area—one level below BASIC)
Select:	File Display Options (from the Options menu)
Type:	*.BAS (in the dialog box)
Press:	[Enter]
Move:	to the File List area
Select:	Select All (from the File menu)
Select:	Move (from the File menu)

Figure B.10

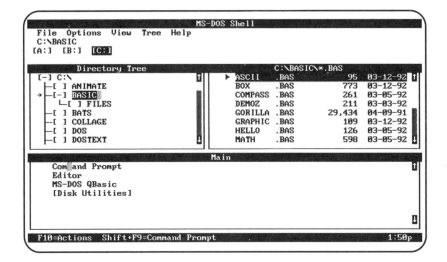

In the To: (of the From: box):

Type: C:\BASIC **(as the destination drive and directory)**

Press: Enter

Notice the File List area displays the message "No files in selected directory," indicating that all of the files were moved.

Now, look at the contents of the BASIC directory by selecting the BASIC directory in the Directory Tree box. The filenames should appear in the File List area and look like *Figure B.10*.

If your screen resembles this, good job!

Renaming Files

Sometimes, you will need to change the names of existing files. For example, if you wanted to use another name for a file, you could designate the new name as the target for a single file. Or, you could also specify, using wildcards, some consistent characteristic in the name of the target (such as .BAK for backup copies of the files).

Let's selectively rename the GORILLA.BAS file (residing in the BASIC directory) to GORILLA.BAK:

Select:	drive C (from the Disk Drive area)
Select:	the BASIC directory (from the Directory Tree area)
Select:	the filename GORILLA.BAS (from the File List area)
Select:	Rename (from the File menu)

The DOS Shell redisplays this dialog box for each file that is renamed; unfortunately, this is a rather slow process.

The DOS Shell should display a dialog box that looks like the one in *Figure B.11*.

Type:	GORILLA.BAK (in the New name. . box)
Press:	[Enter]

The name GORILLA.BAS should be replaced by GORILLA.BAK. To see the file,

Select:	File Display Options (from the Options menu)
Type:	*.* (for all files)
Press:	[Enter]

The names of all of the files—including the renamed file—should appear as shown in *Figure B.12*.

If you prefer, you could type *.BAK to display only files with the extension of .BAK, providing you with the screen in *Figure B.13*.

Figure B.11

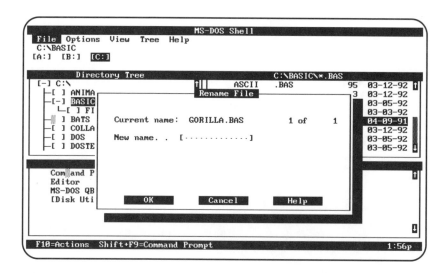

106

Figure B.12

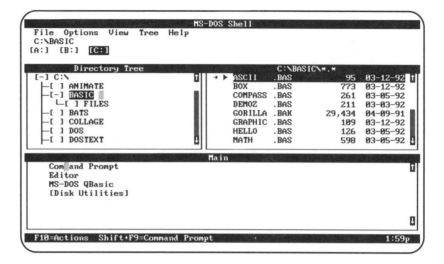

Figure B.13

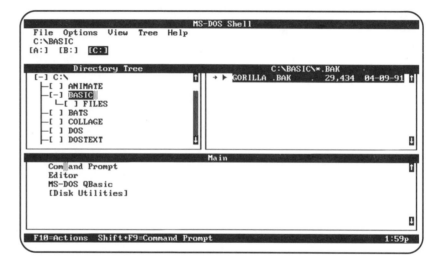

Deleting Files and Directories

The DOS Shell provides you with the ability to delete files and also directories *if the directories contain no subdirectories or files.* It should be stressed that, even though DOS provides you with the capability to delete files, you should consider the consequences very carefully.

107

Let's begin by deleting the files in C:\BASIC (the ones that you copied in a preceding exercise):

Select: drive C (from the Disk Drive area)

Select: the BASIC directory (from the Directory Tree area)

Move: to the File List area

Select: the File Display Option (from the Options menu)

Type: *.* (as the Name: in the dialog box)

Select: the Select All option (from the File menu)

Select: Delete (from the File menu)

You should now have a confirmation dialog box for each file (see *Figure B.14*).

Select the files to be deleted by clicking on OK or YES, or by pressing Enter as each filename is displayed. When all the files are deleted from the BASIC directory on drive C, the message "No files in selected directory" should be displayed.

Now, let's delete both the BASIC and FILES directories.

If you have not completely emptied the directory, the DOS Shell will tell you that it cannot delete the directory until it is empty. This means that you must first remove all of the files and subdirectories from the directory that you want to delete.

Figure B.14

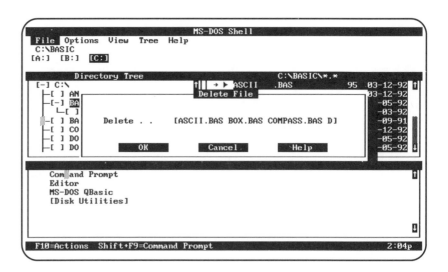

Figure B.15

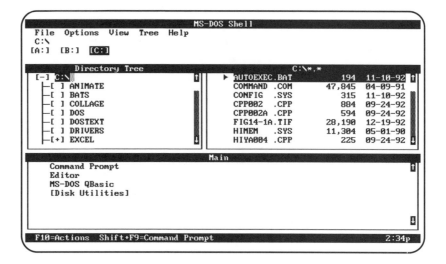

Move: to the FILES directory (in the Directory Tree area)

Select: the Delete option (from the File menu)

Press: ⌜Enter⌝ (to confirm the deletion of the directory)

Now, using the same procedure, delete the BASIC directory. Verify the deletion by checking the Directory Tree area of your screen; it should resemble the one in *Figure B.15*.

Viewing a File's Contents

You may view the contents of a file—and be able to read what you see—if the file is a text file. This means that you cannot comprehend what you see if you attempt to view a .COM or .EXE file because these are executable files and are not readable as text.

Let's see how we can view the contents of a batch (.BAT) file.

Select: the DOS directory of drive C (from the Directory Tree area)

Select: a .BAT file (from the File List area; for example, the previously created backup AUTOEXEC.BAT file from the DOS directory)

109

Figure B.16

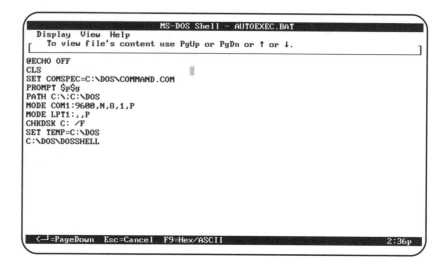

```
                        MS-DOS Shell - AUTOEXEC.BAT
   Display  View  Help
      To view file's content use PgUp or PgDn or ↑ or ↓.

@ECHO OFF
CLS
SET COMSPEC=C:\DOS\COMMAND.COM
PROMPT $p$g
PATH C:\;C:\DOS
MODE COM1:9600,N,8,1,P
MODE LPT1:,,P
CHKDSK C: /F
SET TEMP=C:\DOS
C:\DOS\DOSSHELL




   ←┘=PageDown  Esc=Cancel  F9=Hex/ASCII                              2:36p
```

Select:	**File (from the DOS Shell Menu bar)**
Select:	**View File Contents**

At this time, your screen should show the contents of the selected file—similar to the one in *Figure B.16* (of course, yours will look a little different—depending on the file you chose).

To exit the viewing mode:

Select:	**View (from the Menu bar)**
Select:	**Restore View**

Summary of DOS Shell Techniques

NOTE

DOS command entries are shown in *italics* and are preceded by the word *DOS.*

Desired Result	Action to Take
Change filenames	Select the file and choose Rename from the File menu (*DOS: Rename or Ren*).
Copy files	Press [Ctrl] and drag files to the destination (target), or press [F8], or choose Copy from the File menu (*DOS: Copy*).

Desired Result	**Action to Take**
Create and name a directory	Select the directory (one level above), select Create directory from the File menu, and type the name *(DOS: MD)*.
Delete files	Select the files and choose Delete from the File menu, or press Del *(DOS: Del or Erase)*.
Deselect all files	Press Ctrl-\ or choose Deselect All from the File menu.
Get a list of all files on a disk	Choose All Files from the View menu. *(DOS: Dir)*
Get lists of files from two separate disks or directories	Choose Dual File List from the View menu.
Go to the first or last file in a list of files	Press Home or End.
Move files	Drag them to the new (target) location, or press F7, or choose Move from the File menu *(DOS: Move—version 6.0)*.
Protect a file (make it a read-only file)	Select Change Attributes from the File menu and choose the Read Only attribute *(DOS: Attrib)*.
Search for a filename	Choose Search from the File menu and enter the name of the file. You may also use the * and ? wildcards when searching for a pattern in a filename.
See a list of files in the current directory	Choose Single File List from the View menu *(DOS: Dir)*.

Desired Result	Action to Take
Select a file	Click on it or use the arrow keys to highlight it (in either case, to select a file, it must be highlighted).
Select adjacent files	Hold down Shift and click, or hold down Shift and use the arrow keys.
Select all files	Press Ctrl-/ or choose Select All from the File menu.
Select non-adjacent files	Hold down Ctrl and click. Can also press Shift-F8, use the arrow keys to move to each filename, press Spacebar to select a file, and press Shift-F8 again when finished.
Undelete a file	Choose Undelete from the Disk Utilities in the Main area and give the name of the file to undelete, or press Enter to see a list of files that can be undeleted (*DOS: Undelete*).
View a file's contents	Select the file and then press F9 (*DOS: Type*).

C

Using EDIT as a Text Editor

OBJECTIVES

- Learn how to access EDIT, DOS 5 and 6's full-screen editor
- Use dialog boxes
- Select text to copy, cut, or delete
- Edit and save the

Introduction

Serious personal computer users soon discover that a text editor is a must because this valuable piece of software lets you create text files known as batch files, which allow you to customize and expedite routine tasks. In the past, text editors also provided the faculty for creating simple memos. Today, we have an ample selection of word-processing software that handles this task while providing many more enhancements to the user.

A Brief Comparison With EDLIN

Well-seasoned DOS users are probably familiar with the EDLIN line editor and also know its limitations. One drawback is the necessity to refer to each line of text by a reference or line number. But as of version 5 of DOS, we have EDIT—an editor with no line numbers, just a screen full of text that you can move around. This is referred to as a **full-screen editor.**

However, EDIT won't fill all of your word-processing needs because it doesn't have word wrap, style sheets, character formatting, a spelling checker, a thesaurus, or several other features—but still, it's a great solution for creating and editing short text files.

How to Access EDIT

EDIT can be started either from the command prompt or from within the DOS Shell program. However, EDIT will not start unless the file QBASIC.EXE is in the current directory or unless there is a path to the disk file location where QBASIC.EXE is stored. QBASIC.EXE is an external DOS file; that is, it is not resident in the active memory of your computer. QBASIC.EXE must be retrieved from disk and brought into memory before it can be run (much like the FORMAT file discussed in Lesson 3).

Let's investigate EDIT. At the command prompt,

Type: EDIT/?

Press: [Enter]

and you should see a help screen for this command, as in *Figure C.1.*

Figure C.1

```
12:26
C:\ >edit/?
Starts the MS-DOS Editor, which creates and changes ASCII files.

EDIT [[drive:][path]filename] [/B] [/G] [/H] [/NOHI]

  [drive:][path]filename  Specifies the ASCII file to edit.
  /B          Allows use of a monochrome monitor with a color graphics card.
  /G          Provides the fastest update of a CGA screen.
  /H          Displays the maximum number of lines possible for your hardware.
  /NOHI       Allows the use of a monitor without high-intensity support.

12:26
C:\ >
```

After you read the options for the EDIT command, activate the editor from the command prompt:

Type: EDIT

Press: [Enter]

You should now see EDIT's welcome message *(Figure C.2)*.

To remove this welcome message, simply press [Esc].

Accessing EDIT's Menu Options

EDIT provides you with an easy-to-learn access method. Like any of Microsoft's GUIs (remember, this stands for graphical user interface), you have a menu bar with a good selection of drop-down (or pull-down) menu items and associated options. Now, let's try out some of EDIT's features by accessing the README.TXT data file from the DOS directory.

As the name implies, a README file (sometimes named READ.ME) is a text file that contains additional information regarding DOS. These usually include "hot" items regarding very important—and sometimes technical—aspects of the software.

You are going to open and read the README.TXT file. You need to access the File selection from the Menu bar:

Figure C.2

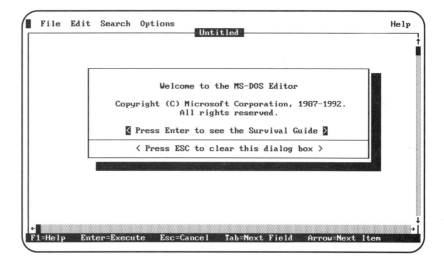

115

Figure C.3

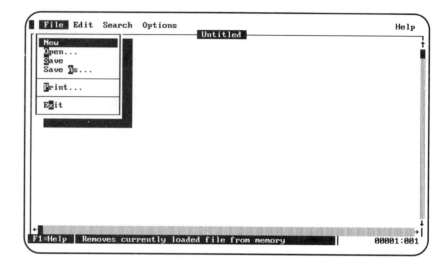

As your DOS skills improve, you will probably find it slower to use the keyboard than to use the mouse—a very good reason to invest a small amount of money in a mouse device.

Press: [Alt] **(or single-click on the word "File")**

The highlighted bar should now be on the word "File."

Press: [Enter] **(to select the File option)**

This should give you a drop-down menu at the top of the screen, as shown in *Figure C.3*.

The highlighted bar should automatically jump to the first item in the menu: the word "New."

Let's review the three separate ways to access a menu item:

- Type the highlighted (capitalized) letter.

- Click on the menu option with the mouse.

- Use the [↑] or [↓] keys to move the highlighter. When it's on the desired item, press [Enter].

You can now select an item as a File menu option. For example, let's select Open, which tells the editor to open or retrieve an existing file from disk. This action should produce a dialog box on your screen, as shown in *Figure C.4*.

116

Figure C.4

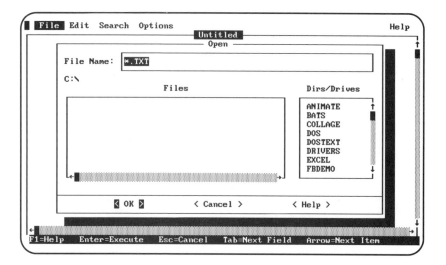

Using Dialog Boxes

NOTE

EDIT always displays *.TXT in the File Name field, but you can type over this with your own file specifications of a filename. Or, you may use the wildcards of a * or the ? (refer to Lesson 5 for details on their use).

As discussed in Appendix A, dialog boxes are used to set options for EDIT commands before the command is actually executed.

The dialog box has five sections. The top line has a box for the File Name. Immediately under that is a line that shows the current directory (in this case, C:\). The Files box is in the middle left portion of the screen. The Dirs/Drives box is on the right. At the bottom of the screen is a section containing the <OK>, <Cancel>, and <Help> options. Moving from section to section is done by pointing and single-clicking or by pressing the [Tab] key (for clockwise movement) or [Shift]-[Tab] (for counter-clockwise movement).

Your screen should still show the File Open dialog box. Now, let's look at the README.TXT file.

First, select the DOS directory in the Dirs/Drives box. To do so,

Move:	to the Dirs/Drives box
Click:	on the word "DOS" (twice)

You may also reach this section of the dialog box with the keyboard:

117

Press: $\boxed{\text{Tab}}$

Highlight: the word "DOS" (use $\boxed{\downarrow}$)

Press: $\boxed{\text{Enter}}$

Notice that the File Name box is updated with the new directory and that the list of .TXT files is displayed in the Files box.

Now, select the filename README.TXT by finding your way to the Files box and selecting the correct filename. Don't forget to either double-click on the name or press $\boxed{\text{Enter}}$ after the name is highlighted.

You can now read the content of the file, scrolling through the text by using the scroll bar (a mouse option) to the right of the screen or by using $\boxed{\downarrow}$ (see *Figure C.5*).

If you are using the keyboard in EDIT, the following key combinations will give you quicker movement on the screen:

$\boxed{\text{Ctrl}}$-C	Page up
$\boxed{\text{Ctrl}}$-R	Page down
$\boxed{\text{Ctrl}}$-W	Move up one line
$\boxed{\text{Ctrl}}$-Z	Move down one line

TIP

You may have to look to the right if there are too many filenames to be displayed in the Files box.

Figure C.5

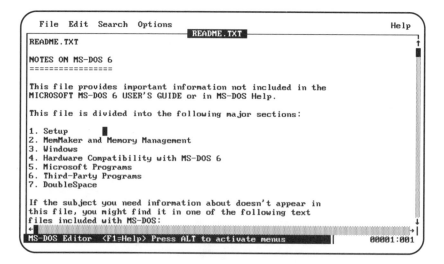

118

For wide documents, use:

Ctrl-Pg Dn   Move one screen to the left

Ctrl-Pg Up   Move one screen to the right

When you are through looking at the text, you can close the file by activating the File option of the Menu bar and selecting Exit from the drop-down menu. This should return you to the command prompt.

Editing Text

We'll look at one more aspect of EDIT, which allows you to edit (change) text.

After the cursor is moved to the position in the text where you want to make a change, you can add, delete, or change the text, one character at a time—or you can mark a block of text and then move, copy, or delete it. When working with a block of text, EDIT places it on a **clipboard** and holds it until you direct EDIT to perform some action with the text (such as to paste it to another location in your document).

Selecting Text to Copy, Cut, or Delete

If you mistakenly highlight too much text, don't despair. To unselect it, you only need to click off of the text or press Esc.

To select text with a mouse, simply point to the beginning of the text, then click and hold down the mouse button as you drag through the text, highlighting it as you go. When you reach the end of the text, release your finger from the mouse button. This may take some practice, so don't be discouraged if you can't master it immediately.

119

Using the Clipboard

Notice the shortcut key sequence to the right of the Edit drop-down menu.

After you've selected a block of text, you may either cut (remove) or copy (duplicate) the block by placing it on the clipboard. You may also, when blocking text, delete the block by pressing the Del key or by selecting Clear from the Edit menu option. To paste the contents of the clipboard to a location within your document, position the cursor in the appropriate location and then select Paste from the Edit menu.

At this time, you should exit EDIT by selecting Exit from the File menu.

For this EDIT exercise, you will edit the AUTOEXEC.BAT file created in Lesson 10. We'll start by loading the EDIT program—and also have EDIT load the AUTOEXEC.BAT in just one step.

Place the diskette that contains the AUTOEXEC.BAT file from Lesson 10 in your diskette drive. Then,

Type: EDIT A:AUTOEXEC.BAT **(if you are using drive B, the A: should be a B:)**

Press: Enter

You should now see the text that you entered when you created your AUTOEXEC.BAT file *(Figure C.6)*.

Figure C.6

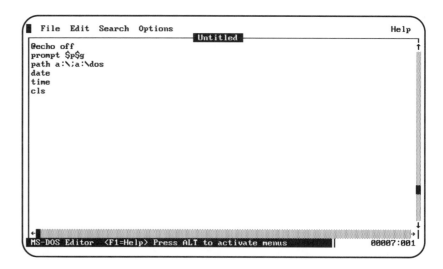

Let's enter a few remark (comment) lines at the beginning of the text. Move the cursor to the leftmost character in line 1 of your text and press Enter; this should create a blank line at the start of your text file.

Now, move the cursor up to the left side of the blank line.

Type: REM A sample file

Press: Enter

Type: REM created by **[your name]**

Press: Enter

Type: REM

Your file should now look like the one in *Figure C.7*.

This revised file is now ready to be saved.

Next, let's check out the cut-and-paste capabilities of EDIT by moving two of the command lines in the AUTOEXEC.BAT file.

Start by moving the cursor down to the leftmost character of line 7, containing the word "date." Now, select the text by either using the keyboard or a mouse.

If you make changes to a file and try to exit the editor, EDIT will ask if you want to save the document before exiting (who said there was no second chance?).

Figure C.7

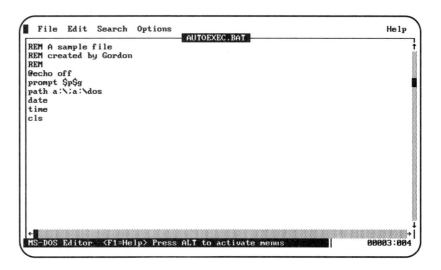

121

Experimenting with the various commands provided by EDIT will familiarize you with the editor—as well as help you build your skills as a GUI user.

Using a keyboard,

Press: ⸢Shift⸥ **and hold it down**

Press: ⸢→⸥ **4 times**

Press: ⸢↓⸥ **once**

Release: ⸢Shift⸥

Using a mouse,

Click: **on the first letter of the word "date" and hold down the mouse button**

Drag: **over the word "date" and down 1 line**

Release: **the mouse button**

Either action should block both the date and time lines.

Next, select Cut from the Edit option of the Menu bar. The two blocked lines should disappear from your screen because they were placed on the Edit clipboard.

Now, we'll insert or paste these lines immediately below line 4 (@echo off) of the file. Position the cursor on the leftmost character of line 5 (prompt pg), select Paste from the Edit option of the Menu bar, and your screen should now resemble *Figure C.8*.

Figure C.8

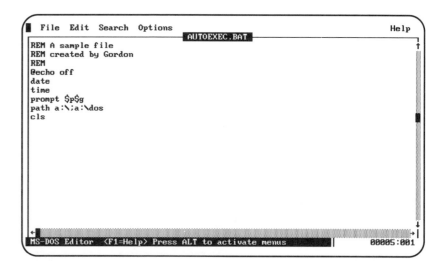

You may choose to save the file under its existing name and location by selecting Save—or you may change the filename and/or location by selecting Save As.

Deleting text is simply done by blocking the text and then selecting Cut from the Edit option of the Menu bar.

This concludes the discussion of EDIT, so let's exit and save the new AUTOEXEC.BAT file by activating the File drop-down menu and selecting the Exit option. You should get a dialog box like the one in *Figure C.9*.

Select the <Yes> option from the dialog box and your file is saved as you exit the editor.

Figure C.9

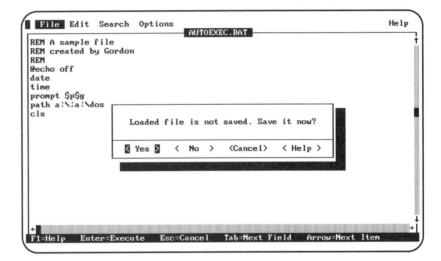

Notes

D

Common DOS Error Messages

Abort, Ignore, Retry, Fail?   A disk error occurred. Type A to end the process, R to retry the operation, or F to end the disk read or write operation. Do not type I because this can cause the loss of data. Earlier versions of DOS do not include the Fail option.

Abort, Retry, Fail?   A diskette device error occurred. Check to make sure that a diskette is in the drive being accessed and that the latch on the drive is closed—then type R for retry. If you cannot correct the problem, type A to abort the process.

Access denied   Access to the file is restricted to read-only status. You may check this status by typing ATTRIB followed by the filename. An "R" should appear to the left of the name, indicating that the file is read-only. (See Lesson 7 for more information.)

Bad command or filename   DOS doesn't understand the instruction that you just entered. Probable cause is one of the following situations: 1) you entered an invalid command (check the spelling), 2) DOS cannot find the command (external DOS command on disk with no path to the file), or 3) the filename specified does not exist, is misspelled, or does not include the 3-digit extension.

Bad or missing command interpreter   The DOS command processor, COMMAND.COM, is not in the root directory of the boot disk, so DOS cannot continue (if booting from a hard disk, make sure floppy drive A is empty). This can be corrected by transferring the system files to the boot disk. Refer to the System (SYS) command in Appendix E.

Cannot move multiple files to a single file   This DOS 6 message means that while using the DOS Move command, you attempted to move more than one file to a single file as a destination. Multiple files can only be moved to a specified drive—or to a specific drive and specified directory.

Check the Mouse Compatibility List   Most likely, your mouse driver is not compatible with DOS 6. Refer to your DOS 6 manual for a list of compatible mouse drivers and procedures to make your mouse driver compatible with the DOS Shell.

Disk error reading (or writing) drive n   This means that the disk (specified by the "n") has a bad sector. Try typing R for retry. If this doesn't do the job, type A to abort.

Disk unsuitable for system disk   An attempt was made to format the diskette as a system disk and a bad track was found where the system files reside. The diskette may not be used as a system disk; however, the diskette may be formatted as a data disk.

Drive not ready error   Normally a result of no diskette in the disk drive or because the door latch is not closed.

Duplicate filename or file not found   You probably tried to rename (REN) a file using an existing filename for the new name. DOS will not overwrite an existing file. Doublecheck the new filename.

File cannot be copied onto itself   The source filename is the same as the target filename. A disk file cannot be copied *over itself*. Check the Copy command and make sure that the target name is different than the source name.

File creation error   Usually a result of using the Copy command to copy or duplicate a file when the filename is already used by a directory; or a file already exists by that name and is read-only; or the disk or directory is full and cannot contain any more files.

Format failure   A fatal disk error prevented DOS from formatting the disk. Do not try to use this disk. Either throw it away or return it for credit (if new). To continue working, format a fresh disk.

General failure   Normally issued when DOS finds an error but cannot give you any specific reason for the error. Check that your disk drive contains a disk, that the disk drive door latch is closed, that the diskette is compatible with the disk drive, and that the diskette was formatted correctly. One of these should remedy your problem.

HIMEM.SYS is missing or not loaded   Check to see if your CONFIG.SYS file contains the correct device=command for HIMEM.SYS and that this command appears before any of the other device commands. The device=command should be similar to:

> `device=c:\dos\himem.sys` (no spaces are allowed in this command)

If your CONFIG.SYS file does not contain this command, then add it and reboot your computer.

Insufficient disk space   You've run out of disk space; the disk is full. Either use another formatted disk (you do have one, don't you?) or delete some of the files from the diskette being used.

Invalid directory   You've incorrectly referenced a directory or you've specified a directory that does not exist. You may have used the CD (change directory) command to incorrectly try to change to another directory. Check the structure of your directories with the Tree command.

Invalid drive specification   You've entered an invalid disk drive letter. Check your typing and make sure that you've included the colon (:) immediately after the drive letter.

Invalid number of parameters   Usually a typing error. The command line did not contain the correct number of parameters for the command that you just entered. Type the keyword of the command followed by /? to ask DOS for help (if you are using DOS version 5 or later).

Invalid path, not directory, or directory not empty   Normally occurs when you are trying to remove a directory. Make sure that you have listed the path correctly, the directory name is spelled correctly, and the directory you are attempting to remove does not contain any files.

Non-system disk or disk error   You've probably tried to start the computer from a non-bootable disk. Maybe you've left a diskette in drive A? Check all your drives and remove any disks that should not be there.

Not ready error reading drive n: Abort, Retry, Fail?   DOS cannot read or write to the disk in the specified drive. Make sure a formatted disk is in the appropriate drive and that the drive door latch is closed.

Out-of-memory   A message displayed due to a shortage of memory while running a DOS-based program. Correct this problem by optimizing your computer's memory. On DOS 6, run MemMaker; on earlier versions of DOS, refer to your DOS manual for instructions on using the HIMEM.SYS driver. Another solution is to disable the loading of other programs, such as TSRs (Terminate and Stay Resident programs), in your AUTOEXEC.BAT file. Also, you might take a good look at your CONFIG.SYS file, cutting it back to specify only files and buffers.

Program too big to fit in memory   DOS is attempting to load an executable program that is too large to be run on your computer. Make sure that you are not running "hot-key" TSRs. If so, delete them—then check the memory allocation by using the Mem command. You may find that you purchased memory (RAM) that was not activated. If so, refer to the source of the add-on memory for instructions regarding how to activate your memory.

Write protect error writing drive n   You've tried to write to a disk that either has a write-protect tab covering the notch on the disk (5¼" diskette) or a write-protect window that is open (3½" diskette). First, you should check to make sure that it's OK to write on this disk. If you still want to write on it, unlock the disk by removing the soft plastic write-protect tab (5¼" diskette) or sliding the hard plastic tab down to close the write-protect window (3½" diskette). Also, some 5¼" diskettes may be read-only; that is, they do not have a notch. In that case, you are not allowed to write on this disk.

Summary of Basic DOS Commands

The following is a summary of frequently used DOS commands. Each command is followed by a brief description, the correct syntax when entering the command, and suggestions on when to use each command. Please note that the disk drive, when required, is followed by a colon (:).

ATTRIB
Versions 3.0 and Later

Displays, sets, or clears a file's read-only, archive, hidden, or system attributes.

To set a file's attributes, use the following syntax:

ATTRIB +R +A +S +H **[drive:][path][filename][/s]**

To clear a file's attributes, use the following syntax:

ATTRIB −R −A −S −H **[drive:][path][filename][/s]**

To display a file's attribute status, use the following syntax:

ATTRIB **[drive:][path][filename][/s]**

- [drive:][path] identifies the drive and directory where the files reside.

- [filename] specifies the file or files (you may use wildcards) to be executed.

- [/s] sets or clears the attributes of the specified files in the current directory and all subsequent directories.

BACKUP
Versions 2.0 and Later

Used to back up one or more files from one disk to another.

BACKUP **[source][target-drive][/s]**

- [source] indicates the location of the files that you want to back up, including the path.

- [target-drive] points to the disk drive to be used for the backup disk(s).

- [/s] tells DOS to back up the contents of all subdirectories.

CD (CHDIR)
Versions 2.0 and Later

Used to display or change the current directory.

CD **[drive:][path]**

- [drive][path] identifies the location of the directory you want to display or change.

CHKDSK
Versions 1.0 and Later

Used to display information about a specific disk or directory. Displays the number of files, how many bytes of storage space are unused, whether there are lost clusters (fragmented files), and similar information.

CHKDSK **[drive:][path][filename][/f][/v]**

- [drive:][path] identifies the drive, directory, or files you want to check.

- [filename] is a valid DOS filename (wildcards are permitted).

- [/f] tells DOS to convert any lost clusters that it discovers into temporary files.

- [/v] displays the name of each file that DOS checks.

CLS
Versions 2.0 and Later

Clears the screen and redisplays the DOS system prompt.

COPY
Versions 1.0 and Later

Used to copy one or more files.

COPY **[source file(s)][destination file(s)][/v]**

- [source file(s)] indicates the files that you want to copy, including the path.

- [destination file(s)] indicates where the files should be copied to (wildcard characters can be used for multiple files).

- [/v] tells DOS to verify that all files were copied correctly to the destination location.

DATE
Versions 1.0 and Later

Used to display or change the system date. You respond with the time in the form *mm-dd-yy,* with *mm* the month, *dd* the day, and *yy* the year (for example, 06-15-93).

DEL (ERASE)
Versions 1.0 and Later

Used to erase a specific file or group of files.

DEL **[drive:][path][filename][/p]**

- [drive:][path] identifies the drive, directory, or files that you want to delete.

- [filename] is the name of the file or files you want deleted (wildcards are permitted).

- [/p] tells DOS to prompt you to verify deletion before actually deleting a file.

DIR
Versions 1.0 and Later

Displays a listing of all files in a specified directory. For example, type DIR C: to list all the files in C:.

DISKCOPY
Versions 2.0 and Later

Used to create an exact duplicate copy of a diskette (with the same size and capacity). Reformats the target disk. Will not work on hard disks.

DISKCOPY **[drive1][drive2][/l][/v]**

- [drive1] specifies the source disk.

- [drive2] specifies the destination disk.

- [/l] specifies that only the first side of a two-sided diskette should be duplicated.

- [/v] tells DOS to verify the duplication process.

DOSKEY
Versions 5.0 and Later

This command, when activated, maintains a log of the commands that you type and allows you to play back the command list. Typing DOSKEY directs DOS to load and activate the DOSKEY program in memory. You can then recall the list and reexecute commands that you previously typed. You can also edit the command list. The most basic form of this command is:

DOSKEY

Typed with no parameters, this command tells DOS to install the DOSKEY program with 512 bytes of memory—enough to record about 25 DOS commands (each approximately 20 characters long).

DOSSHELL
Versions 4.0 and Later

Used to start the DOS Shell.

EDIT
Versions 5.0 and Later

Enables you to use a full-screen text editor, giving you much the same capabilities of a very simple word processor.

EDIT **[filename]**

- [filename] specifies the name of the file to be created or edited (changed). When creating a new file, the filename may be omitted; instead, it may be specified when saving the file.

EDLIN
Versions 1.0 and Later

A line editor. The only DOS edit program available before DOS version 5.

> EDLIN **[filename]**

- [filename] specifies the name of the file to be created or edited (changed).

ERASE

See DEL (ERASE)

FORMAT
Versions 1.0 and Later

Prepares a disk to be used by a DOS-based computer (refer to Lesson 3 for details).

> FORMAT **[drive:][/v:label][/f:size][/s][/1][/4][/8]**

- [drive] specifies the drive in which the disk to be formatted is located.

- [/v:label] assigns *label* as a volume label to a formatted disk with DOS 4 and later. With DOS versions prior to 4, /v (without "label") tells DOS to prompt for a volume label after formatting is complete.

- [/f:size] specifies the capacity, in kilobytes, for which the diskette should be formatted with DOS 4 and later. Valid sizes are 160, 180, 320, 360, and 720 kilobytes, plus 1.2, 1.44, and 2.88 megabytes.

- [/s] creates a system disk by copying DOS system files to the formatted disk.

- [/1] formats one side of a 5¼" diskette for use on older computers.

- [/4] formats 5¼" 360KB diskettes in a 1.2MB drive (used primarily with DOS versions prior to DOS 4).

- [/8] formats 5¼" diskettes with 8 sectors per track for use on older computers.

HELP
Versions 5.0 and Later

Beginning with version 5, DOS provides online help with command formats. Requesting help for a particular command causes DOS to display a description of the command and the correct syntax for the command—with a list and description of all parameters for the particular command.

Help can either be requested by typing:

HELP **[command name]**

or by typing:

[command name]/?

- [command name] in either case is the name of the command for which you are requesting help.

LABEL
Versions 3.1 and Later
(PC-DOS Releases 3.0 and Later)

The Label command allows you to display, add, change, or delete the volume label of a disk. If you do not enter the volume label as part of the disk formatting process, you may assign a volume label by using the DOS Label command.

LABEL **[drive:] [new label]**

- [drive:] specifies the drive containing the disk to be labeled.

- [new label] is the volume label that you will want to assign to the disk in [drive:]. If the [new label] parameter is omitted, DOS will prompt you for it during the labeling process.

MD (MKDIR)
Versions 2.0 and Later

Used to create a new directory or subdirectory on disk.

MD **[drive:] [path]**

- [drive:] specifies the drive on which you want the new directory created.

- [path] is the pathname for the new directory.

MOVE
Version 6.0

This command allows you to move one or more files to the location that you specify. The Move command may also be used to rename directories. Moving a file to an existing file overwrites the existing file. If you are moving more than one file, the destination name must be a directory name.

MOVE **[drive:][path][filename],[drive:][path][filename],...
[destination]**

- [drive:][path] specifies the drive and directory containing the file to be moved.

- [filename] specifies the name of the file to be moved.

- [destination] can consist of a drive letter and colon, a directory name, or a combination of both. If you are moving a single file, you can specify a new name for the file in order to rename it during the move process.

PATH
Versions 2.0 and Later

Used to display or specify a command search path.

PATH **[drive:][path];[drive:path];...[drive:path]**

- [drive:][path] is the list of drives and directories to be included in the search path (note the ; separator between multiple locations).

PRINT
Versions 2.0 and Later

Prints a text file.

PRINT **[drive:][path][filename][/c][/t]**

- [drive:][path] identifies the location of the file you want to print.

- [filename] specifies the name of the file to be printed.

- [/c] cancels printing of the specified filename.

- [/t] removes all files from the print queue.

135

PROMPT
Versions 2.0 and Later
(PC-DOS Releases
2.1 and Later)

Allows you to reset the system prompt.

PROMPT **[prompt options]**

- [prompt options] allows for customization of the prompt. The typical options are pg, which indicates the default drive followed by the display of the current directory, followed by the > symbol (for example, PROMPT pg yields a prompt like C:/DOS>, indicating a default of the DOS directory on drive C). Refer to Lesson 9 for more information.

RD (RMDIR)
Versions 2.0 and Later

Allows you to remove a directory or subdirectory. A directory or subdirectory cannot be removed until all files and subordinate directories are deleted from within the directory to remove.

RD **[drive:][path]**

- [drive:] specifies the drive on which the directory to remove resides.

- [path] is the pathname of the directory to delete.

REN (RENAME)
Versions 1.0 and Later

Used to rename a file or a particular group of files.

REN **[drive:][path][oldfilename(s)] [newfilename(s)]**

- [drive:][path][oldfilename(s)] specifies the location and name of the file to rename.

- [newfilename(s)] specifies the new name(s) for the file(s). Wildcards may be used with this command.

RESTORE
Versions 2.0 and Later

Restores files that were backed up by using the Backup command.

RESTORE **[source][target-drive][/s]**

- [source] specifies the drive on which the backup files are stored.

- [target-drive] specifies the location to which the files are to be restored.

- [/s] restores all files in all subdirectories.

SYS
Versions 1.0 and Later

Copies the command processor (COMMAND.COM) and the hidden files to a formatted disk, making the disk into a bootable disk. Creating a bootable floppy disk is important when setting up a new PC because this gives you a way to start up the system if you make a mistake with the hard disk (such as accidentally formatting C:). For example, type SYS A: to make the disk in drive A into a bootable disk.

TIME
Versions 1.0 and Later

Allows you to check or set the current system time.

    TIME

You respond with the time in the form *hh:mm:ss,* with *hh* the hour (add 12 to hours after 12 noon), *mm* the minutes, and *ss* the seconds (if you're quick enough!). For example, 7:31 P.M. (and 45 seconds) is entered as 19:31:45.

TREE
Versions 3.2 and Later
(PC-DOS Releases
2.0 and Later)

This command shows the structure of a disk or directory by displaying the directory and subdirectory names and, optionally, the names of the files in each directory. Versions 4 and later provide a more comprehensive graphic display of the diagram.

TREE **[drive:][path][/a][/f]**

- [drive:] identifies the drive to be referenced.

- [path] is the path to a specific directory. If you omit the path, DOS displays the current directory of the specified drive.

- [/a] uses ASCII instead of extended characters.

- [/f] displays the names of the files in each directory.

TYPE
Versions 1.0 and Later

Used to display the contents of a text (ASCII) file.

TYPE **[drive:][path][filename]**

- [drive:][path][filename] identifies the location and the name of the file to be displayed.

UNDELETE
Versions 5.0 and Later

The Undelete command allows you to restore files deleted by the Delete or Erase command. When used, this command replaces the files on the drive and in the directory from which they were removed.

Although Undelete can save you considerable time and agony when you inadvertently delete crucial files, you cannot always undelete a deleted file. When DOS deletes a file, it tags the disk file storage space as available for reassignment. In other words, DOS may have already given the disk space to another file, overlaying your old file with other data—making the deleted file unrecoverable. For this reason, you should undelete a file as soon as possible and you should be extremely cautious when deleting files.

UNDELETE **[filename][/dt][/dos][/all][/list]**

- [filename] is the name of the file or files that you want to restore. You may specify a drive and path, as well as use the wildcards of * and ? to indicate a specific group of files.

- [/dt] tells Undelete to recover deleted files recorded by the delete-tracking function of the Mirror command (refer to your DOS manual for use of the Mirror command).

- [/dos] tells Undelete to prompt you for confirmation before deleting a file.

- [/all] tells Undelete to recover all files without stopping and requesting confirmation.

- [/list] tells Undelete to display a list of files that can be undeleted. Unrecoverable files are marked with a double asterisk (**).

UNFORMAT
Versions 5.0 and Later

Lets you undo a disk format by recovering files and directories after an accidental format. However, UNFORMAT cannot restore a disk formatted with the /U parameter of the Format command.

UNFORMAT **[drive:]**

- [drive:] identifies the drive referencing the disk to be unformatted (this may be a hard disk).

VER
Versions 2.0 and Later

Allows you to display the version (release) of DOS currently running on your system.

VOL
Versions 2.0 and Later

Displays a disk volume number (versions 4 and later also display the serial number).

> VOL **[drive:]**

- [drive:] is the drive containing the disk whose volume label will be displayed.

XCOPY
Versions 3.2 and Later

Copies files (except hidden and system files) and directory trees.

> XCOPY **[source files(s)][destination file(s)]**
> **[/d:date][/m][/p][/s or /s/e][/v]**

- [source file(s)] indicates those files you want to copy, including the path.

- [destination file(s)] indicates where the files should be copied to (wildcard characters may be used for multiple files).

- [/d:date] copies files changed on or after the specified date.

- [/m] copies files with the archive attribute set and turns the archive bit off.

- [/p] prompts you before creating each target file.

- [/s] copies directories and subdirectories (except empty ones).

- [/s/e] copies *all* subdirectories (even empty ones).

- [/v] verifies each new file.

139

Glossary of Terms

A> or A:\> DOS prompts indicating that the default drive is floppy drive A.

Archive status the archive status attribute [a] marks files that were changed since they were previously backed up.

ASCII pronounced "Ask-ee." An acronym for American Standard Code for Information Interchange. A coding scheme that uses values from 0 to 127 to represent numbers, letters, and symbols that are used by a computer. In DOS, ASCII typically refers to a plain, unenhanced text file.

ATTRIB the command used to display or change a file's attributes, indicating a file's status within the DOS filing system. The four attributes are archive, hidden, read-only, and system.

Attributes are file settings that allow you to control access to a file. Attribute settings also can be used to show the backup status of a file or to indicate system files. Attributes are set with the Attribute (ATTRIB) command.

AUTOEXEC.BAT a file that DOS automatically runs each time that you boot your PC.

Backup used in reference to backing up files. A method of copying a specified number of files (many times, a complete disk) to a series of diskettes. DOS provides both Backup and Restore commands for this purpose.

BIOS Basic Input/Output System. These are the programs that control the PC's input and output devices.

Booting   the process of turning on the computer and loading DOS into the computer's memory. A cold boot is, as the name implies, a start by turning on your PC's switch or switches—usually after the computer has been turned off for awhile (and is cold). A warm boot or reboot is easier on your equipment: while the computer is already on (warm), hold down the [Ctrl] and [Alt] keys and press the [Del] key—then release all three keys.

Buffer   an internal (RAM) area of storage used to temporarily hold data.

C> or C:\>   DOS prompts indicating that the default or referenced drive is drive C. This is the normal reference for the hard disk.

Check boxes   check boxes appear to the left of the options available in a given dialog box. To select (or deselect) an option, single-click in its check box.

Clicking   quickly pressing and releasing the mouse button (normally the leftmost button).

Clipboard   a reserved portion of the computer's memory that holds data until you want to perform some action on it.

Command buttons   buttons found in most dialog boxes that tell the DOS Shell what to do next. The most common Command buttons are OK, Cancel, and Help.

COMMAND.COM   the DOS command processor that contains *internal* DOS commands (such as COPY and DIR).

CON   the DOS name for the keyboard.

CONFIG.SYS   this file allows you to customize your system configuration. Such tasks as installing device drivers, setting limits on files and buffers, and carrying out DOS high-memory allocation occur within this file.

Context sensitive   when using the DOS Shell Help utility, this means that Help is sensitive to the task you are currently performing and provides you with related on-line information.

Cursor   the blinking dash on the screen. This shows where the next text that you type will start.

Data disk   diskette on which you normally save data files, such as word-processing or spreadsheet documents.

Default drive   also referred to as the current drive. It is the active disk drive whose letter is shown in the DOS prompt (such as A> or C>).

Dialog box   a screen window, used by the DOS Shell, that prompts you to provide the information necessary to complete a command.

Directory   a collection of disk files. Files may be saved to disk in various directories. Subsequent directories are sometimes referred to as subdirectories. The DIR command allows you to view file lists of disk files.

Directory tree   a diagram that shows the structure of the directories on a specified disk drive.

Disk   a storage device—referred to as either a hard disk or as diskettes (floppy disks)—used as secondary storage for files of information. Diskettes come in two sizes: $5\frac{1}{4}$" and $3\frac{1}{2}$", each with either a standard- or high-density capacity. It is important to match the disk (density) to the type of disk drive.

DOS   the Disk Operating System for your computer. DOS is the controlling program for your PC and all of its components. It also provides you with the ability to use disks and files.

DOSKEY   a command to start a program that allows you to recall commands that you previously entered.

DOS Shell   the software that lets you perform many DOS commands using menus and—if you choose to—a mouse.

Double-clicking   used to activate an item, this is done by pointing to the object, then pressing and releasing the left mouse button two times, very fast.

Dragging   pressing and holding down a button while moving a mouse.

EDIT   this command starts the DOS editor, which lets you create or "work over" the contents of an ASCII file.

Executable file a file whose instructions are executed or run when the filename is typed. DOS filenames with extensions of .COM, .EXE, and .BAT are executable DOS files.

Extension three characters used to identify the type of file. Typically, .DOC and .TXT extensions are used for text files; .EXE and .COM for program files. Names cannot contain spaces or certain special characters. File extensions are always separated from the root by a period.

External command a DOS command that is not included in COMMAND.COM; it is stored on disk. To use an external command, the command must either be located in the current directory of the default drive, or DOS must be told where to access it.

File a collection of data saved to disk. The file could be output (such as a spreadsheet, word-processing document, or a graphics image).

File allocation table (FAT) a table created by formatting and used by DOS to keep track of disk space usage and files.

Filename a filename consists of the root (1–8 characters) plus a 3-digit extension. The extension is preceded by a period (such as .TXT). Do not use filenames that have special meaning (for example, Copy or Delete).

Floppy disk a PC's removable disk that is inserted into a 3½" or 5¼" disk drive. A floppy disk is composed of oxide-coated mylar stored inside a square envelope.

Formatting a process that prepares a diskette to make it usable by your PC. This is done by using the DOS Format command.

Full-screen editor a text editor that allows you to move around the screen as you edit a document, making changes as you go.

Graphical user interface (GUI) allows you to use the mouse in conjunction with the keyboard to manipulate on-screen images (called menus and icons) to perform a chosen DOS task.

Hard copy the printed copy.

Hard disk the fixed disk inside your PC. This device has a large capacity (measured in megabytes) and is much faster than using a diskette drive. A typical hard disk has a 40-, 80-, or 120-megabyte capacity. If the hard disk is too small, it may be replaced with a larger one (for more money, naturally).

Hardware the physical parts of your PC, like the nuts and bolts in a hardware store.

Hidden files files that exist, but are not visible on a directory listing. This is accomplished by setting the "H" attribute.

Icons on-screen images displayed as pictorial representations of items, such as a file cabinet for the selection of the DOS file function.

Internal command a DOS command (for example, Dir) included in COMMAND.COM. When DOS is booted, COMMAND.COM becomes active in memory (RAM). Since an internal command resides in memory, it may be accessed without concern for the default prompt or path.

KB or kilobyte a thousand bytes. Actually, one KB is equivalent to 1,024 bytes (to be exact); therefore, 640KB are equivalent to $640 \times 1,024$ or 655,360 bytes.

List box an area found in many dialog boxes that displays a list of items, such as filenames, from which you may select one or many of the items.

Literal any sequence of alphabetic and numeric characters. A literal is placed after the Prompt command to manipulate the prompt.

MB or megabyte one million bytes (or 1,024 kilobytes).

Memory the temporary storage where the computer keeps the data that is currently being accessed (such as a document that you are preparing when using a word processor). This is sometimes referred to as RAM, standing for Random Access Memory. This differs from ROM, which stands for Read Only Memory.

Menu a screen display of options available in a computer program.

Metastring a text string placed after the Prompt command to manipulate the prompt. The text string normally contains a dollar sign ($), followed by a special character.

Mouse   a pointing device used to manipulate items when operating in graphics modes, such as with the DOS Shell. The leftmost button on the top of the mouse is normally clicked to get a response from the computer. However, if you are left-handed, the rightmost button may be activated instead (this is usually done at setup, install, or configure time).

Mouse droppings   this occurs when you move the mouse and see the cursor scattered across the screen, typically in the path behind the mouse. This is caused by a program neglecting to turn off the mouse at the proper time. The solution is to reboot your computer.

Mouse pointer   a pointer that may be used to control the cursor, maneuver objects on the screen, or execute a program. Character-oriented programs generally have little use for this device, but graphics programs find it a must.

MS-DOS   an abbreviation for Microsoft Disk Operating System, this is the standard operating system for IBM-compatible micro-computers. Also known simply as DOS.

Option buttons   used with a DOS Shell to turn options off or on.

Parameter   an argument or limit that can be used with a DOS command. An example of a parameter could be the source and target drives associated with the Copy command.

Pathname   the name that includes the drive letter, a colon, the directory, and the filename. This is the exact location of a file to be accessed. For example, C:\DOS\FORMAT tells the PC to run the file named FORMAT that resides in the directory named DOS on disk drive C. Note that the pathname may be omitted from the command line if the path was previously set by the Path command (in this case, to the directory named DOS).

PC-DOS   the IBM PC version of MS-DOS.

Personal computer (PC)   the smallest of the computer family, equipped as a total system of hardware and software to be used in the home, office, or just about any other place.

Pixel   one of hundreds of dots on your PC's display screen. This item is very important when displaying images or graphics. Much like your TV screen, more pixels produce a sharper picture because the individual pixels display the color to create images. When you purchase a monitor, you specify the type of screen and the number of pixels—the more, the better.

PRN the DOS name for the system printer.

Program a set of organized, logical instructions that direct a computer to perform a given task.

Prompt the DOS prompt is typically a C:\>, indicating that the default or referenced drive is drive C. If your PC's prompt is either an A> or a C> (without the colon and backslash), then refer to Lesson 9 on setting the prompt; this is important when working from the command line.

Queue a list of files to be processed.

RAM stands for Random Access Memory. This is your computer's primary memory. It temporarily stores the data that you are currently working on.

Read-only status this status is set by the Attribute command and provides for protection from accidental deletion of files.

ROM Read Only Memory. A special chip that contains code or instructions for your PC. This code can be accessed, but not changed. A PC's BIOS (Basic Input/Output System) is stored on a ROM chip.

Root the first (name) part of a filename. A root may contain from 1–8 characters, which may be followed by an extension. For example, SAMPLE is the root in the filename SAMPLE.DOC.

Root directory every disk drive has a "parent" or root directory—which in turn has "children" or subdirectories. The root directory is typically displayed as the drive letter and a \ (backslash) in a disk's directory listing.

Scroll to continuously move upward or downward through a list of items on the screen.

Scroll bar a long narrow bar typically at the right side of the DOS Shell screen. This bar contains a small box and arrows at the top and bottom, which you use to scroll (or "look") through a list of items on the screen.

Shell   a program that insulates you from DOS by allowing you to perform operations using the graphical user interface (GUI).

Single-clicking   used to select items, this is done by pointing to an item on the screen and then pressing and releasing the left mouse button once.

Software   the set of programs, procedures, and related documentation associated with a computer system. Examples of software include DOS, word-processing programs (such as WordPerfect), and spreadsheet programs (such as Lotus 1-2-3).

Source   the original from which you make a copy. You normally copy files *from* the source *to* the destination (the target).

String   like a string of text, this is a group of characters or words (any non-numeric data).

Subdirectory   a directory that is below the root or another directory; normally, just referred to as a directory.

System attribute   [s] designates a file as a system file. Files with the system attribute are not shown on directory listings, but can be seen by using the Attribute command.

System disk   a disk that is formatted to contain the DOS command processor and the DOS hidden system files. You can boot the PC with this diskette.

Target   the destination (for example, of a copying operation). A target may be a filename, directory, or disk drive.

Text box   a box used by a DOS Shell, which allows you to provide information (such as a filename for editing).

Text editor   a very basic word processor that lets you add, delete, and edit text in the ASCII format.

Version   a specific release of a software package (for example, DOS 6 is the sixth main version of a long line of DOS versions and sub-versions). Each main version (such as 4.0) introduces substantial changes and improvements from the previous versions. Each sub-version (such as 4.01) fixes smaller items that did not work properly in the previous version.

Volume label   an optional name (up to 11 characters) that may be used to identify a disk. This label information is written by DOS to the disk as a data file. The label may be entered or changed by using the DOS Label command.

Wildcards   in DOS, the asterisk (*) and the question mark (?), which allow you to specify several files by using one command.

Write-protect   locking a diskette so that the information contained on it may be read—but not changed, erased, or written over. On a 3½" disk, this is done by sliding a hard plastic tab and opening the small window in the corner. On a 5¼" diskette, you place a special tab over the write-protect notch that is cut into the upper-right side of the diskette. Make sure that you *do not use anything except a special write-protect tab*. Ordinary tape can gum up—or even destroy—your disk drive.

Index

? (question mark) as a wildcard
    character, 37–38
* (asterisk) as a wildcard character,
    37–41
: (colon) as a drive letter suffix, 9
/ (slash)
    with command switches, 8
    used with Help utility, 134
    versus backslash, 8
... (ellipsis), with command options,
    87–88
\ (backslash), in directory
    commands, 8

A> or A:\> prompt, 4, 6, 141–148
alphanumeric, 141–148
archive status, 55
ASCII, 83, 141–148
ASSIGN command, 76
ATTRIB command, 51–52, 129
AUTOEXEC.BAT file, 73, 141–148

backslash (\), in directory
    commands, 61
backup
    described, 141–148
    files, 43–44
    options, 44–45
BACKUP
    command, 44, 130
    examples, 48–49
.BAT extension, 20–21, 74
batch files, 74
BIOS, 4
bit, 141–148
boot, 141–148
bootable floppy disks. See system
    disk
booting your computer
    cold boot, 4
    warm boot, 4
BREAK command, 76
buffers, 32, 141–148

BUFFERS= command, 76
    See also CONFIG.SYS command
byte, 141–148

C> or C:\> prompt, 4, 6, 141–148
case sensitive, 8
CD (CHDIR) command, 61, 130
changing directories, 61
changing the prompt. See PROMPT
    command
CHDIR (CD) command, 61, 130
CHKDSK command, 130
clearing your screen, 10
clicking the mouse, 83–84, 141–148
clock, 10
CLS command, 10, 131
CMOS, 141–148
cold start (boot), 4, 141–148
colon (:) as a drive letter suffix, 9
.COM extension, 20–21
COMMAND.COM file, 3, 141–148
command line, 141–148
command listing (DOS), 129–139
command processor, 3
commands
    See internal commands
    See external commands
    See specific command of interest
compatible, 141–148
CON, 30, 141–148
CONFIG.SYS file, 73, 76–77, 141–148
coprocessor, 141–148
COPY command, 31, 131
copying
    an entire disk, 34–35
    files, 31–32
    with 1 disk drive, 34–35
    with 2 disk drives, 34
CPU (central processing unit),
    141–148
creating a bootable (system)
    diskette, 23–25
creating directories, 59

current directory, 61
current drive. See default drive
cursor, 4, 141–148
cut, 119
cursor keys, 141–148
customizing your prompt, 71

DATE command, 10, 131
dates
    displaying at DOS prompt, 10–11
    entering today's, 11
default, 141–148
default drive, 5
DEL command, 131
deleting
    directories, 63
    files, 64
density of floppies, 22
dialog box, 87–88, 141–148
DIR command, 12–18, 132
directory (subdirectory)
    command, 12–18, 132
    creating, 59–60
    deleting, 63–65
    described, 141–148
    display, 5
    display and pause at the end of a
        page (/P), 14
    selecting, 61–63
    single disk label, 25
    tree, 141–148
    using, 57–58
    wide (/W), 15
disk
    capacity, 22
    defined, 141–148
    See also floppy disk capacities
DISKCOPY command, 34, 132
display, 141–148
displaying a directory, 12
DOS
    command line, 141–148

Index

commands. *See* specific
   command of interest
  described, 141–148
  filenames, 19–20
  loading from floppy-disk
   systems, 5
  loading from hard-disk systems, 5
  Shell, 141–148
DOSKEY command, 132, 141–148
DOSSHELL command. *See also* Shell
  defined, 80, 132
  directories
   creating, 97–99
   deleting, 108–109
   selecting, 94
  drives
   selecting, 94
   using, 93
  files
   copying, 101–102
   deleting, 107–108
   moving, 103–105
   nonsequential, 96
   renaming, 105–107
   selecting, 95
   sequential, 95
   viewing contents of, 109–110
dot matrix, 141–148
drop-down menu, 87

ECHO command, 75
EDIT command
  accessing, 114
  clipboard, 120–123
  compared to EDLIN, 113–114
  copying text, 119
  cutting text, 119
  defined, 132
  deleting text, 119
  dialog boxes, 117–118
  help, accessing, 114
  menu access, 115
  using, 113
ellipsis (...), 87–88
Enter (Return) key, using with
  commands, 5
error messages, 125–128
.EXE extension, 20–21
executable instructions, 20
external commands, 4
external files, 39

FAT (file allocation table), 23
file attributes
  archive, 51
  hidden, 54
  read-only, 52
  system, 55
file names
  creating, 19–20
  described, 141–148
  extensions, 20, 141–148
  root, 20
  using wildcards, 37
FILES= command, 76
floppy disks
  capacities, 22
  defined, 21, 141–148
  formatting, 23
  systems, 5
FORMAT command, 24–27, 133
formatting
  data disk, 25
  described, 141–148
  lower density disk on a higher
   density drive, 26–27
  options, 26–27
  system (bootable) disk, 23–24
full screen editing, 141–148
function keys, 141–148

Glossary of Terms, 141–148
groups of files
  copying, 101–102
  deleting, 108–109
  moving, 103–105
  renaming, 105–107
  selecting with keyboard, 95
  selecting with mouse, 96
GUI (Graphical User Interface), 79

hard copy, printing, 32
hard-disk drives. *See also* disks
  defined, 141–148
hardware, 1, 141–148
HELP
  command, 134
  from the Shell, 91
hidden files, 52, 54, 141–148
highlighting, 82, 88, 95–97
hyphen (-) as collapsible-directory
  indicator, 100

icons, 80
I/O, 141–148
internal clock, 10
internal commands, 4

KB (kilobyte), 141–148

LABEL command, 134
labeling disks, 46
limiting access to files, 51
literals, 70
loading DOS
  floppy-disk systems, 5
  hard-disk systems, 5
looking at a file's contents, 30
lowercase, 141–148

making copies of files, 29
MB (megabyte), 141–148
MD (MKDIR) command, 59, 134
memory
  defined, 141–148
  RAM (random access memory),
   12, 141–148
  ROM (read-only memory),
   141–148
memory-resident programs, 141–148
menu bar, 80
menus, drop-down, 87
metastrings, 70
microprocessor, 141–148
military time, 10
minus sign (–) as a
  collapsible-directory indicator,
  100
MKDIR (MD) command, 59, 134
MORE command (filter)
  See use with TYPE command,
   inside back cover
mouse
  defined, 141–148
  double-clicking, 84
  dragging, 84
  single-clicking, 84
  using, 79, 83–85
MOUSE.COM, 84
MOUSE.SYS, 84
MOVE command, 135
moving. *See* DOSSHELL command
MS-DOS. *See* DOS

MS-DOS Shell. *See* DOSSHELL command

naming
   directories, 59
   files, 19–20
numeric entry, 141–148

online help. *See* HELP command
option buttons, 141–148

parameters, 8
parallel port, 141–148
PATH command, 66–67, 135
path names, 39, 65–67, 141–148
pausing (/P) when displaying
   directories, 14
PC, 141–148
PC-DOS. *See* DOS
peripheral, 141–148
piping (|) symbol.
   See use with DIR and TYPE
      commands, inside cover
pixel, 141–148
plus (+) as compressed-directory
   indicator, 100
port, 141–148
PRINT command, 135
printing a copy of a file, 32
PRN, 32, 141–148
program, 141–148
prompt
   changing, 9
   command, 69–70
   customizing, 71–72
   defined, 4, 141–148
   string, 70
PROMPT command, 70, 136

queue, 141–148
question mark (?), 37–38

RAM (random access memory), 12,
   141–148
RD (RMDIR) command, 63
read-only status, 52
REM command, 121
REN (RENAME) command, 136
Restore
   Command, 47

Options, 47–48
restoring backed up files, 43, 47
RESTORE command, 136
Return (Enter) key, using with
   commands, 5
RMDIR (RD) command, 63
ROM (read-only memory), 141–148
root directory, 58, 141–148

scroll, 141–148
secondary storage, 23
serial port, 141–148
setting a path, 65
setting the system date and time, 10
setting your system prompt, 69
shell elements
   box jumping, 85
   cascading menus. *See* Drop-down
      menus
   check boxes, 88–89
   check mark, 88
   command buttons, 89
   described, 141–148
   dialog boxes, 87–88
   disk drive area, 82
   drop-down menus, 88
   ellipsis, 88
   file menu, 80
   help
      asking for, 91
      menu, 81
   list boxes, 88–89
   main display area, 82
   menu bar, 80
   menu bar activating, 86
   mouse
      double-clicking, 84
      dragging, 84
      single-clicking, 84
      use, 83
   option buttons, 88–89
   options menu, 81
   scroll bars, 85
   text boxes, 88–89
   tree menu, 81
   view menu, 81
   Windows, Microsoft, 80–81
slashes (keyboard), 8
software, 1
SORT filter. *See* inside back cover
source, 141–148

source file, 31
status line, 80
string, 141–148
subdirectories, 57, 141–148
syntax, 141–148
SYS command, 137
system disks (bootable), 23, 55,
   141–148

target, 141–148
target file, 31
text box, 141–148
text editor, 141–148
time
   displaying at DOS prompt, 10–11
   entering current, 10–11
TIME command, 10, 137
title bar, 80
TREE command, 62, 137
tree menu, of DOS Shell menu bar,
   81
tree structure of directories, 62
TYPE command, 30, 138

UNDELETE command, 138
undeleting a file, 112, 138
UNFORMAT command, 27, 139
unformatting a disk, 27
upgrading your DOS, 8
upper case letters, 59

VER command, 8, 139
versions of DOS, 2–3, 8
vertical bar (|). *See* piping symbol
VOL command, 139
volume label, 24

warm boot, 4
wildcards, 37, 141–148
wide format (/W) for directory
   listings, 15–16
Windows program, Microsoft, 20
write-protecting a disk, 12–13,
   141–148

XCOPY
   command, 32–33, 139
   examples, 33

About the Author

A computer professional since the early '60s, Gordon Kimbell was employed by General Telephone as a programmer, systems analyst, and in a variety of management positions before joining Everett Community College as an instructor of Computer Information Systems in 1967. While employed as an instructor, Gordon has taught programming as well as microcomputer courses in operating systems, spreadsheets, and databases. Throughout his college employment, Gordon has returned to industry several times in order to keep pace with current technologies.

During the 1988-91 academic years, Gordon held the position of Instructional Computer Coordinator for the State of Washington Community College System. He was also the director of Academics at the National Computer Educators' Institute at Western Washington University for the summers of 1990 and 1991.

He enjoys fishing, running, and many outdoor activities. Gordon and his wife Arlene make their home in LaConner, Washington, in the heart of the beautiful Skagit Valley.